GET A GRIP

Facing Life's Toughest Challenges

DR. DAVID C. COOPER

GET A GRIP: Facing Life's Toughest Challenges

ISBN: 0-924748-64-8
UPC: 88571300034-5

Printed in the United States of America

Milestones International Publishers
4410 University Dr., Ste. 113
Huntsville, AL 35816
(303) 503-7257
www.milestonesintl.com

1 2 3 4 5 6 7 8 9 10 11 / 09 08 07 06 05

ENDORSEMENTS

In *Get a Grip*, Dr. David Cooper meets people where they are...dealing with the everyday, real issues of life. In simple yet powerful language, he shares straightforward solutions, rooted in timeless biblical truths, to tackle and conquer these problems. His words provide an inspirational blueprint to confront these challenges and to live more fully in the will of God.

Sonny Perdue
Governor of the state of Georgia

Dr. Cooper has done it again. This book is filled with both practical research and spiritual insight that anyone can apply to their life. Whether you spend time in a board room, a class room or a play room with children—this book will become a friend as you negotiate the challenges of stress, guilt, worry, depression, anger and other hurdles we face in our lives. You won't regret soaking up this book!

Dr. Tim Elmore
President, GrowingLeaders.com

In his book, *Get a Grip: Facing Life's Toughest Challenges*, Dr. David Cooper presents a down to earth, with-God's-help-you-can-do-it approach to living out the Christian life in joy and victory.

In this day of negativism and global turmoil, when fear is the face of the world, this is a book that will both inform and inspire for courageous living regardless of the circumstances.

Paul L. Walker, Ph.D.
President
Ministry Now Concepts

David Cooper's *Get a Grip* instructs those of us living in a hectic world how to keep God at the center of our lives, experience joy, dream big dreams, and achieve great things. Cooper is like a great spiritual and mental coach sharing a game plan for victorious life. You will not only enjoy this book, it will enrich and transform your own journey.

Ralph Reed
President, Century Strategies
Former Executive Director, The Christian Coalition

CONTENTS

1. Get a Grip on Stress 1
2. Get a Grip on Grief 15
3. Get a Grip on Depression 25
4. Get a Grip on Guilt 41
5. Get a Grip on Anger 55
6. Get a Grip on Circumstances 67
7. Get a Grip on Change 79
8. Get a Grip on Priorities 91
9. Get a Grip on Worry 101
10. Get a Grip on Decisions 113
11. Get a Grip on Time 125
12. Get a Grip on Perfectionism 137

About the Author 153

1

GET A GRIP ON STRESS

My wife Barbie and I were walking in Yosemite National Park when we passed a guy wearing a T-shirt which read: "Caution: Contents under Great Pressure." I turned to her and said, "I need a T-shirt like that!"

We all feel like that at times, don't we? Pressure on the outside—stress on the inside. Stress is no respecter of persons. From the multi-millionaire to the child in school, we all experience stress from a host of pressures.

Stress is a state of mental, physical and emotional tension. It can be defined as the wear and tear our bodies experience as we adjust to a changing environment. Such anxiety, in modest amounts, keeps us motivated. But too much stress is toxic.

Prolonged stress contributes to heart disease, high blood pressure, stroke, cancer, and other illnesses. It weakens the immune system, which protects us from many serious diseases. Tranquilizers, antidepressants, and anti-anxiety medications account for one fourth of all prescriptions written in the United States each year. Nearly half of all American workers suffer from symptoms of burnout, a disabling reaction to stress on the job. An estimated one million workers are absent on an average workday because of stress-related issues, and an estimated 40 percent of worker turnover is due to job stress.

One study concluded that unmanaged reactions to stress were a more dangerous risk factor for cancer and heart disease than either cigarette smoking or the consumption of high-cholesterol foods. Up to 90 percent of all visits to primary care physicians are for stress-related complaints. As many as 80 percent of industrial accidents are due to stress. And over 50 percent of lost work days are related to ever-increasing levels of job stress. Stress-related disorders cost American businesses over $150 billion annually.

What causes stress? One survey found the following causes: 36 percent said that work was the primary cause of personal stress; 32 percent identified financial pressures; 10 percent said that children caused them the most stress; 7 percent said it was ill health; 5 percent said it was their marriage; and 5 percent said their parents caused them stress. Only 5 percent said they had no stress, and 19 percent said they had little stress.

How do we handle stress? 40 percent of women say that at times stress at work causes them to eat chocolate. (Now there's an excuse!) Two female scientists were talking about stress one day in a lab at UCLA. One joked to the other that when the women who worked in the lab were stressed, they came in, cleaned the lab, had coffee, and bonded with one another. When the men were stressed, they retreated somewhere on their own. They noted that almost 90 percent of the research on stress had been done on males, and decided to launch a new study focusing on women.

The results of their landmark study, recently published, suggest that women respond to stress with a cascade of brain chemicals that cause women to make and maintain friendships with other women.[1] Previous research had suggested that stress triggers a hormonal response that prepares the body to either stand and fight or flee as fast as possible. It now appears that women's brains function differently than men's in reaction to stressors. According to the study, women tend to respond by releasing a hormone called oxytocin. This hormone causes them to engage in what the scientists call "tending and befriending" behavior; that is, caring for children or gathering with other women. This behavior in turn generates more oxytocin, which counters stress and has a calming effect.

Stress is a major issue today. We can barely pick up a magazine or turn on the news without hearing about new ways to combat it. We know, for instance, that nutrition, exercise and rest are vital in properly handling stress. Is there anything else that might help? I believe there is one very powerful tool to help each one of us.

The greatest antidote to stress is the peace of God. Only God can give us true and lasting peace. *"The LORD will give strength unto his people; the LORD will bless his people with peace"* (Psalm 29:11, KJV). The prophet Isaiah said that God will keep us in *"perfect peace"* when our minds are fixed on Him and because we trust Him (Isaiah 26:3-4). Jesus said, *"Peace I leave with you; my peace I give you"* (John 14:27).

The greatest antidote to stress is the peace of God.

But if Jesus left us a legacy of peace, why do we so often fail to possess it? I was talking to a close friend about a message I was to deliver on the subject of peace. He said I should entitle it, "If God Gave Me Peace, Where Did I Put It?" This seems to be the dilemma of far too many Christians!

You see, a promise and the possession of a promise are two different things. We can only live in perfect peace if we learn to practice peace. When Jesus said, *"My peace I give you,"* He meant that He had already taught His disciples to live by faith the principles that produce peace. Let's look at some lessons from Jesus' own experience with stress on keeping your peace. The following account occurred on the Sea of Galilee, which is prone to sudden violent storms.

> *That day when evening came, he said to his disciples, "Let us go over to the other side." Leaving the crowd behind, they took him along, just as he was, in the boat. There were also other boats with him. A furious squall came up, and the waves broke over the boat, so that it was nearly swamped. Jesus*

was in the stern, sleeping on a cushion. The disciples woke him and said to him, "Teacher, don't you care if we drown?"

He got up, rebuked the wind and said to the waves, "Quiet! Be still!" Then the wind died down and it was completely calm.

He said to his disciples, "Why are you so afraid? Do you still have no faith?"

They were terrified and asked each other, "Who is this? Even the wind and the waves obey him!"

Mark 4:35-41

KEEP GOD AT THE CENTER OF YOUR LIFE

How could Jesus be at such peace during the storm? His secret was simple: He kept His Father at the center of His life. We can do that by keeping God at the center of our thoughts, decisions and actions. We need to focus on the changelessness of God's love and faithfulness rather than on our stressful circumstances. Things in life change, but God remains the same. His love endures forever!

That is why Jesus could sleep during a life-threatening storm on the open sea. He knew that storms come and go, but God remains the same. Prayer keeps us focused on God; the release of our feelings to God in prayer brings peace. Prayer is more than asking God to give us things, or to do things for us. Prayer is about solitude, being alone with God, focusing on His presence. Solitude and stillness in the presence of God bring a deep sense of reassurance that He is not going to abandon us or let us fall.

Jesus often withdrew to solitary places to pray (e.g., Luke 5:16). We know that when we are alone and quiet, negativity decreases; alertness, calmness, creativity and energy increase. I recently called the home of friend who had just been released from the hospital after having had brain surgery for cancer. I was shocked when he himself answered the phone. He has fought six battles with cancer; yet as we talked, his faith in God was radiant. I called to lift him up, but he lifted me up with his triumphant attitude! Why? Because he focused on his Creator, not on his cancer.

A survey was conducted by the National Opinion Research Center. They questioned Americans who had recently suffered divorce, unemployment, bereavement, or serious injury or disability. Their major finding was that those who had strong faith retained a greater sense of joy in life.[2] Other studies, reported by Dr. David Meyers in his book, *The Pursuit of Happiness*,[3] show that those who participate regularly in worship consistently exhibit a greater ability to manage the stresses of aging and personal crises. Religious people (defined by most studies as those who attend church or synagogue regularly) are less likely to abuse drugs and alcohol, to divorce or be unhappily married, or to commit suicide. They also tend to be physically healthier and to live longer. "Religious faith buffers the negative effects of trauma on well-being," says Duke University sociologist Christopher Ellison.

DETERMINE TO REACH YOUR DESTINATION

Jesus knew God would get Him to His destination regardless of the storm. He had determined to go to the other side of the sea, and He fully believed He would get there. Likewise, you can use your stress to motivate you to press on toward your goals.

Peace accompanies a focused mind. It's when we have a "double mind" that the soul is troubled. *"A double-minded man* [is] *unstable in all he does"* (James 1:8). It is fear that keeps us from our destination. We want to reach the other side of our own Seas of Galilee. The other side for us may be a financial goal, a business pursuit, a relationship issue or a personal concern. But fear keeps us stuck where we are. A mind clouded by fear is not focused; how can the goal be reached if it is not clearly seen? A person with a focused mind has ceased questioning and doubting; he knows beyond a shadow of a doubt that the goal can be reached! When Jesus told His disciples, *"Let's go to the other side,"* He had every confidence that God would keep Him safe until He reached His destination. We need to have the same confidence in God. That's what keeps us in perfect peace when the storms of life rage.

Salvatore R. Maddi, professor of psychology at the University of California, Irvine, and president of the Hardiness Institute, says that it is the hardiest of people who best handle stress. Hardiness is that group of characteristics that make people try to solve problems rather than fall victim to them. It is unrealistic for any of us to think we can have stress-free lives. The important thing is to resolve stressful problems when they arise by turning them into opportunities. Maddi offers three C's:

Commitment to being active in life rather than sitting back and letting events and circumstances define one's life and position.

Control, or trying to influence outcomes instead of being passively influenced by them.

Challenge, or learning from both positive and negative experiences.[4]

CLEAR YOUR MIND OF WORRY

Dr. Charles Mayo once commented that half the hospital beds are filled with people who worry themselves there. *Peanuts'* Charlie Brown sometimes seems to be headed in that direction. He and Linus were sitting around talking one day. Charlie said to Linus, "I worry about school a lot." He thought a little longer and then said, "I worry about worrying so much about school." Upon further reflection he concluded, "My anxieties have anxieties!"

In our passage from Mark about Christ and the storm, something should stand out: Jesus was asleep on a pillow. Nothing in the Bible appears by accident. Every word is intentional and filled with meaning. Jesus must have taken a pillow with Him. The lesson is clear—wherever you're going, take a pillow. What do I mean by that? The pillow is a symbol of Jesus' inner attitude of faith. He was resting in the hands of God. And that is what we need to do.

Don't overlook the most obvious lesson: Get plenty of rest. Sufficient rest is vital to handling stress. Many people today are experiencing sleep deprivation. Research in this area shows that most people need nine hours of rest each night for maximum efficiency. Sleep deficiency is related to depression, mood swings, fatigue, lack of concentration, anger and rage reactions, and memory loss.

The fact that Jesus took a pillow meant that He expected to be at peace. Jesus was sleeping on a pillow when His disciples woke Him up. He was at peace—they were having a panic attack. Jesus must have been in a deep sleep: His friends had to try to wake Him up! The tossing of the boat, the sounds of the storm, the cries of the men—none of these were sufficient to wake Him. Don't you hate it when someone wakes you up out of a deep sleep? I'm sure Jesus was irritated, too. But He turned immediately to His Father's work in meeting the needs of those around Him.

In order to sleep well, you need to free your mind of worry and guilt. These are the two great enemies of peace of mind. Decide that you are not going to live in fear and guilt, but in faith! *"Do not be anxious about anything, but in everything, by prayer and petition, with thanksgiving, present your requests to God"* (Philippians 4:6).

Whenever the poet Amy Lovell stayed at a hotel, she had to rent five rooms: one on either side so that she did not hear any noise, one across the hall so that no one disturbed her rest by coming in and out the door noisily late at night, and one on the floor beneath hers so that she wasn't hearing any sounds from underneath. That's the only way she could have a peaceful night's sleep! Charles Dickens, the great author, could not sleep until his bed was laid along a north-south axis; only then did he sleep deeply.

The American National Institute of Mental Health reports that there are 200 types of sleeping tablets available to help people sleep. Worry is a contributing factor in high blood pressure, arthritis, heart disease and ulcers. One study of 450 people who lived to be a hundred years old or older found that these people lived long for the following reasons: They kept busy; they practiced moderation in all things; they ate lightly and simply; they got a great deal of fun out of life; they were early to bed and early to rise; they were free from worry and fear, especially fear of death; and they had serene minds and faith in God.[5]

REBUKE THE STORMS

When Jesus arose from sleep and saw the storm, He simply rebuked it and it died down. He spoke to the storm. He didn't accept things as they were, but He changed them by His word of faith. If you say something long enough, you'll believe it. Our words have a great impact on our attitudes and actions.

Jesus rebuked the storm. He was active, not passive, in the face of His unpleasant circumstances. We are often too passive with our problems, believing that we are doomed to have them or that they will go away on their own. But you've got to take charge of your circumstances and decide that living in a state of constant stress is unacceptable.

I spoke recently with a man who has been in rehab from a stroke for two years. Sitting in his wheelchair, barely able to move the left side of his body, he explained that his doctor had told him he had done all he could do. His response? "That's unacceptable." He told me, "My condition is unacceptable. I will never give up trying to get better and working hard at therapy." He's rebuking his storm!

It's time for you to speak to the mountain that's standing in your way, blocking you from reaching your destination. Jesus said we could move a mountain by speaking words of faith (Matthew 17:20-21). *Rebuke* is a word used often within Jesus' ministry. He rebuked demons. He rebuked the Pharisees for their self-righteousness. He rebuked His disciples for their unbelief (Matthew 17:17). He even rebuked Peter for his self-centeredness (Matthew 16:23).

We are to imitate Christ. But how should we imitate His rebukes? What should we rebuke? Start by rebuking the negative statements you have grown up believing. Say, "By the grace of God, I will not live in defeat, but in victory." Anything in life that you are willing to put up with will probably be a persistent problem. But if you dare to rebuke it, you can calm your storm and move your mountain. The Bible itself is useful for rebuking negative and destructive thoughts.

You also need to rebuke any negative labels, such as loser, addict, trouble-maker or lazy, that may be keeping you in bondage. You can declare, "I rebuke the label of

______, and I confess that I am the righteousness of God in Christ Jesus" (see Second Corinthians 5:21).

Rebuke negative people and don't listen to negativism, criticism and complaint. When people try to fill your mind with their negative attitudes, explain that you don't have time to listen to such things. Your mind is not a trash can into which people, the culture and the media are free to dump their useless trash. Your mind is the sanctuary of God.

Rebuke your problems. Declare by faith, "I will not keep living in this condition. I will change my world and my circumstances by God's power in me!" Faith is the victory that overcomes the world. Speak to the mountain! Rebuke the storm today and every day until it dies down.

SPEAK TO YOUR CIRCUMSTANCES

Jesus declared to the storm three words: *"Peace, be still."* Say those three words out loud. Go to the office early tomorrow and walk around the workplace of stress and say, *"Peace, be still."* Go into the bedroom when your children are sleeping and say to them, *"Peace, be still."*

Words impact thoughts, emotions and behavior. *"I believed, therefore I have spoken"* (Second Corinthians 4:13). Speak peacefully to others and to yourself. It has been pointed out that it is impossible to yell at someone who is whispering to you. *"A gentle answer turns away wrath, but a harsh word stirs up anger"* (Proverbs 15:1).

After Jesus spoke these words—*"Peace, be still"*—the wind died down and all was completely calm.

You are the master of your own circumstances because God is with you as He was with them.

FOOD FOR THOUGHT

1. What are the things in your life that cause you the most stress?
2. Have you prayed about these areas, giving them over to the Lord? Do you think that would be an appropriate response?
3. What does it mean to "take your pillow" into a situation? Can you think of a time when you were able to do this? Is there a place in your life right now where you should take your pillow?
4. What are some Scriptures that can help you manage stress in your life?

2

GET A GRIP ON GRIEF

Columbine. 911. Tsunami. Katrina. Words that elicit feelings of grief on a global scale.

Divorce. Terminal illness. Bankruptcy. Failure. Death of a loved one. Experiences filled with grief on a personal level.

Grief is a feeling of sadness associated with the loss of someone or something we love. The death of Pope John Paul II was met with masses of people gathering around the world to express their grief. Yet death is a tragedy repeated on the personal level all too often: Every day 155,399 people die, including 35,000 children. And grief is not only felt in times of the death of a loved one; for instance, every day in America 7,000 couples get divorced, affecting 10,000 children with the death of the marriage.

Loss comes to us in many ways. The only way to handle grief is to draw near to God, where we find comfort and strength. We hold dear His word: *"Come near to God, and God will come near to you"* (James 4:8). He also promises, *"I will turn their mourning into gladness; I will give them comfort and joy instead of sorrow"* (Jeremiah 31:13).

Let's look at a biblical account which teaches us how to deal with feelings of grief. The prophet Samuel was paralyzed by it. Saul, the first king of Israel, had started the monarchy well, but ended in colossal failure. Samuel's selection and anointing of Saul looked to him to have been one big mistake. He would learn that good decisions can go sour if people mismanage what God has given them. The Lord regretted that He had made Saul king. He commissioned Samuel to tell Saul that the kingdom was being taken from him and given to a man after God's own heart. Samuel faithfully delivered the message, but fell into the trap of grief and depression.

The only way to handle grief is to draw near to God, where we find comfort and strength.

Then God spoke to the prophet in his grief and gave him a message *apropos* to us:

> *The LORD said to Samuel, "How long will you mourn for Saul, since I have rejected him as king over Israel? Fill your horn with oil and be on your way; I am sending you to Jesse of Bethlehem. I have chosen one of his sons to be king.*
>
> First Samuel 16:1

The end result of Samuel's obedience would be the calling of David to reign as the new king of Israel.

HOW LONG WILL YOU MOURN?

God called Samuel to move through the grief process to resolution. Grief takes time. The question is, "How much time?" A popular theory, first propounded by Dr. Elizabeth Kubler-Ross, holds that there are five stages of grief: denial, anger, bargaining, depression and acceptance.[6] However, more recent studies are showing that this progression of the stages of grief does not hold true for everyone. The fact is that people handle grief in unique ways. Not everyone goes through these five stages.

We can feel lost in the wilderness of grief. Life is on hold while we are paralyzed in our depression, anger, sadness, confusion and pain. There is an appropriate time for grief, for grief is a vital part of life. It cannot, nor should it be, rushed. Well-meaning people may tell us to "move on"; yet we need time to grieve and to heal. On the other hand, we cannot afford to allow grief to be the final chapter of our life. There comes a time to pick ourselves up and keep going.

Grief can cripple us. When God asked Samuel how long he would mourn for Saul, it touched on Samuel's feelings of failure. Samuel was the one who had anointed Saul as the first king of Israel. Saul became a terrible leader and died in defeat. Samuel felt that Saul's demise was a reflection of his own inadequate leadership. After all, he himself had appointed Saul; no other man was involved. Now, Samuel's own ministry was on hold. Was there more he could have done for Saul? Did he pray enough? Was there something he could have said to make Saul a success instead of a failure? I'm sure he wrestled with these questions. We too blame ourselves for the failures of others when we have invested much in them.

Grief can turn to bitterness, hopelessness and cynicism if not resolved. Such was the case of Naomi, whose name means "pleasant." She became so bitter from grief that she changed her name to Mara because, she said, *"the Almighty has made my life very bitter"* (see Ruth 1:20-21).

How is grief resolved? Through joy!

We see this in our response to sin. Sin results in guilt, which brings about feelings of grief. We feel like failures in the sight of God. While guilt may be redemptive in the sense that it leads us to confront our sins and seek God's forgiveness, it can also cripple us if we don't accept the joy of that forgiveness. We are to mourn over our sins, but then we are to receive by faith God's forgiveness and rejoice that we are loved and forgiven. *"The joy of the LORD is your strength"* (Nehemiah 8:10).

FILL YOUR HORN WITH OIL

After God asked Samuel how long he planned to stay in mourning, He gave him some instructions: *"Fill your horn with oil, and go."* Why was Samuel to do that? Because God still had a purpose for him. Although the prophet could not see it because of his grief for what did not work out, God still had a plan; He was still in control. You see, the oil contained within the horn was that which the prophet would use to anoint the next king. To *anoint* is to consecrate for a spiritual calling. The oil would be poured on the top of the head of the person being consecrated and it would then drip off the head onto the shoulders, covering the person's garment. The oil represented the Spirit of God coming upon the person, empowering him for the work to which God was calling him.

When grief strikes, we need a fresh experience of God.

God will give us a new infilling of the Spirit to help us move from grief to a new purpose in life. *"After they prayed ... they were all filled with the Holy Spirit and spoke the word of God boldly"* (Acts 4:31). We too can pray and God will fill us with His Holy Spirit, giving us new boldness and courage to face the challenges of life.

The horn into which the prophet poured the oil represents strength. We see that Samuel later traveled to the home of Jesse in the town of Bethlehem. When he met young David, he *"took the horn of oil and anointed him in the presence of his brothers, and from that day on the Spirit of the LORD came upon David in power"* (First Samuel 16:13). Grief leaves us fatigued, exhausted, running on empty. But the Holy Spirit gives us new power and strength to do what God has called us to accomplish in life.

When grief strikes, we need a fresh experience of God. It is hard to worship when we're struck with grief and all its baggage. We need to go the house of God for spiritual renewal or take time alone with God, that He might refill the horn with oil. When David battled grief over the result of his moral failure, he went to the house of God to worship. Later, he wrote of God, *"You anoint my head with oil; my cup overflows"* (Psalm 23:5). When God gives you a fresh anointing of His Spirit, your cup of joyous energy will overflow.

Lou Gehrig, the "Iron Horse" of baseball, long held the record for the most consecutive baseball games played at 2,130 games. Sadly, he suffered from amyotrophic lateral sclerosis, a progressive neuromuscular disease that came to bear his name. In his book *They Rose Above It,* Bob Considine tells of the day Lou Gehrig called him from his office. Mayor LaGuardia had appointed him to the New York City Parole Board to work with and encourage young men who were in trouble with the law. Gehrig devoted himself fully to the work with everything he had, or had left. He also kept up a lively interest in research into the disease that had driven him out of baseball.

"I've got some good news for you," Lou told Bob. "Looks like the boys in the lab might have come up with a real breakthrough. They've got some new serum that they've tried on ten of us who have the same problem. And you know something? It seems to be working on nine out of ten. How about that?" Lou was elated.

Bob writes, "I tried not to ask the question, but it came out anyway. 'How about *you,* Lou?' "

Lou said, "Well, it didn't work on me. But how about that for an average? Nine out of ten! Isn't that great?" I said, yes. It was great. So was he.[7]

BE ON YOUR WAY, FOR I AM SENDING YOU

What was the last thing God told Samuel to do to get over his grief? *"Be on your way, for I am sending you."* That's a nice way of saying, "Get on with it!" Grief may last for a season; but there comes a time to move on to the next season. You cannot spend your life trying to improve the past. I believe life is like writing a book. Sometimes you have to close a chapter and start a new one. No one gets to start over; life doesn't come with a rewind button. You have to start where you are and build for the future. God has a new opportunity waiting for you.

This word from God marked a call for Samuel to be productive in his ministry. And He wants the same thing for each one of us. Don't sit idly by when you battle grief—be on your way, for God is sending you! How do we go forth on our way? I believe there are three stages necessary for us to move on. We must get a vision, develop a plan of action, and get going.

First, you need to gain a new vision. In other words, you have to develop a mental picture of where you want to go before you can begin your journey. *"Where there is no vision, the people perish"* (Proverbs 29:18, KJV). Everything begins with vision. What do you see ahead for yourself? For your family? For your business? For your career? Samuel overcame his grief by knowing that God was still sending him. God never gives up on us. He always has a purpose for us. Even if you have failed, the gifts and callings of God are still upon your life. Ask God to reveal to you His purpose and plan.

When the prophet Jeremiah sat in prison, he thought his purpose was over. But God spoke to him and gave him a new vision for his life:

> *While Jeremiah was still confined in the courtyard of the guard, the word of the LORD came to him a second time ... "Call to me and I will answer you and tell you great and unsearchable things you do not know."*
>
> Jeremiah 33:1, 3

You too can break out of the prison of grief by calling on God and getting a new vision for your life.

Secondly, you need to develop a plan of action. A vision without a plan of action is simply a good idea going nowhere. God promises to direct our steps if we will take the next step. *"The steps of a good man are ordered by the* LORD*"* (Psalm 37:23, KJV). God will not show us everything we are going to experience. Who could handle knowing the future? God expects us to walk by faith. If you trust God with your life, you will have no interest in knowing the future, because you understand that *"in all things God works for the good of those who love him"* (Romans 8:28).

Samuel did not know ahead of time who the next king would be, yet he was a great prophet! Nevertheless, he started moving the day God spoke to him. Only after he began to walk in obedience did God direct his steps to Bethlehem so that he would meet a shepherd named Jesse. And only when he had met eight of Jesse's sons did the Holy Spirit reveal to Samuel that David would be the new king. The will of God unfolds one step at a time when we take the first step of faith. You must take action steps if you want God to direct your life. *"The steps of a good person are ordered by the LORD."* It is in taking steps, not standing still, that our lives are ordered.

Finally, it is important to get started ... today! I am sure Samuel wondered whether his next appointment of a king would end in failure, as it had with Saul. His fear of failure could have kept him from doing God's will. Yet he walked forward in obedience to the vision God gave him. Even so, we have to rise above the fear of failure and of being hurt if we expect to enjoy life. Fear is a prison. If you are in it, it's time for a jail break! If you're not, then stay out of it by acting in faith in the face of your fears. Do the thing you are afraid of and fear will be conquered.

Here is God's positive message to help us get a grip on grief:

> *"How long will you mourn? Fill your horn with oil and be on your way, for I am sending you!"*

FOOD FOR THOUGHT

1. Are you experiencing a time of grieving? What is the source of your feelings of grief?
2. If you have not brought these things to the Lord, please take time now to do so, giving each concern and source of grief into His hand.
3. What are the three stages necessary for moving out of grief? Which stage are you on? What can you do to move on to the next step?
4. Look for any Sauls in your life—failures or stumbling blocks that have caused you to stop moving forward in God's purposes for you. Ask the Lord to forgive you for any failures on your part, and to help you to move beyond the Sauls to the Davids in your life.

3

GET A GRIP ON DEPRESSION

Eric Atkinson. Recognize the name? Probably not. He was little known outside his own circle. His life was not one an outsider would point to as being filled with significance.

Yet his death was. Eric Atkinson was the 1,000th person known to have leaped to his death from the Golden Gate Bridge in San Francisco since the bridge opened in 1937.

Suicide is one of the worst possible outcomes of depression. When I preached at a revival service in northern Georgia a few years ago, a young couple came to me in distress. Her brother had taken his life; the church they attended told them he had definitely lost his soul because suicide is an unpardonable sin. But this is not true! When people commit suicide, they are not thinking clearly. God is a merciful God who knows the condition of our hearts and of our minds.

Depression has been called the common cold of emotional suffering. It is an often temporary emotional state of extreme sadness, which ranges in intensity from mild to severe. The incidence of depression has more than doubled in the last 50 years in the U.S. Almost 20 million Americans suffer from it at any given time, and twice that will suffer it in their lifetime. Women suffer from depressive disorders at twice the rate of men. One in four women will suffer from depression in her lifetime. By the year 2010, depression will be the second most common health problem in the U.S., just after heart disease. A Massachusetts Institute of Technology study showed that depression costs the American economy $43.7 billion a year ($20 billion in treatment costs and $23.7 in lost productivity and absenteeism).[8]

The World Presidents' Organization, comprised of top business executives, estimates that 25 percent of top-level executives experience depression at some point in their careers. Yet ninety percent of these executives never seek help. Successful people are often thought to be superhuman, without any problems. Since depression is often seen as a weakness instead of a disease, these businessmen never ask for help due to fear of losing their positions.[9]

Teenage depression is one of the most common illnesses among adolescents, and teen suicide is among the leading causes of death for that age group. The National Institute of Mental Health (NIMH) estimates that up to 8 percent of teens suffer from major depression; girls are twice as susceptible as boys. According to a

1999 survey, about 20 percent of high school students have seriously considered suicide; and every year 8 to 11 out of every 100,000 teens succeed in ending their own lives.[10] The teen suicide rate has tripled in the last few decades. Part of the reason for this may be that teen depression is often misdiagnosed. While adults tend to internalize their negative feelings, teens act on their aggressions. Depressed teenagers may become angry or defiant. They may act irresponsibly and often turn to alcohol or drugs to relieve their depression, only to be left in deeper despair. Any teen who has experimented with drugs should be checked for signs of depression.

What are the symptoms of depression? Emotionally we may feel hopeless, worthless, guilty, angry, anxious, and irritable. We lose motivation. Intellectually, we think negatively, become pessimistic, suffer memory loss, have difficulty concentrating, grow indecisive and, in chronic depression, entertain thoughts of death or suicide. Physically, we lack energy, feel fatigued and tired, lose interest in pleasurable activities, have significant changes in appetite or weight, and are unable to accomplish tasks or work. We may either lose sleep or oversleep as an escape mechanism. Socially, we withdraw and isolate or become overly dependent on others. Spiritually, we feel estranged and cut off from God. Even Moses, Job, Elijah and Jonah, all of them great men of faith, battled depression; and many of David's psalms express his bouts with this malady. There are three experiences in the Christian life: mountaintop experiences of great blessing, victory and excitement; ordinary days filled with routine living; and dark days of discouragement and depression.

Why do we become depressed? It is often the result of a body chemistry imbalance caused by trauma, illness, hormonal changes, substance abuse, lack of sunlight and other causes.

We need a mindset of hope inspired by the promises of God.

How can we escape depression? Medication helps to stabilize people with severe, chronic depression that is chemically-based. Yet with or without medication, attitude change is a must in overcoming depression. A study at the University of Pennsylvania, Philadelphia, reveals how cognitive therapy can be as effective as antidepressant medication when it comes to treating depression. Cognitive therapy involves helping a person "unlearn" negative thinking patterns and beliefs and replace them with more constructive ideas.[11]

We need a mindset of hope inspired by the promises of God. Hope says, *"With man this is impossible, but with God all things are possible"* (Matthew 19:26).

Motivation and hope can make all the difference. For instance, a man was walking home one night, taking a shortcut through a graveyard. It was very dark, so he didn't see the newly dug grave that lay in his path. He fell headlong into it. When he regained his senses he tried to crawl out, but the ground was wet and slippery. Finally he gave up and sat down in the corner. Thinking that surely someone would help him out in the morning, he fell asleep. About an hour later, another man came walking through the cemetery. He too fell into the grave. He tried to climb out, but he couldn't make it out, either. However, all of the noise he made in his attempts woke the first man, who had been sleeping in the corner. Realizing what was going on, the first man said to the second, "Hey, you can't get out of here. I've already tried." But guess what? Hearing that voice coming from the grave, that man was motivated! And he got out!

The Scriptures record an ancient song about depression sung by the Israelites when they were in captivity in Babylon, which today is Iraq. The song reveals powerful truths about the causes, symptoms and cures for depression.

> *By the rivers of Babylon we sat and wept when we remembered Zion. There on the poplars we hung our harps, for there our captors asked us for songs, our tormentors demanded songs of joy; they said, "Sing us one of the songs of Zion!" How can we sing the songs of the LORD while in a foreign land?*
>
> Psalm 137:1-4

WE SAT DOWN

When depression strikes, we sit down. We quit because we feel fatigued and tired. We lose our motivation as we give in to hopelessness. What is the answer?

We need to stand up! Function whether you feel like it or not. Say, "I am going to work today depressed. I am going to worship depressed. I am going to get my education depressed."

There's a fascinating story in the Old Testament about four lepers (see Second Kings 7:1-9). Lepers are people who suffer from the chronic disease known as leprosy, which causes a wasting away of body parts. Lepers suffered great rejection in the ancient world. Their appearance in a public place brought great fear. They were forced to live outside the cities in leper colonies.

The events of this account took place around 850 B.C. The Aramean (Syrian) army had surrounded Samaria under King Ben-Hadad. Eventually all the food ran out and the people were starving. All hope was lost. The Aramean forces were camped a few miles away, awaiting the city's surrender. Meanwhile, four lepers sat, ignored, outside the city gate. These four men decided to take action.

This is where faith begins to operate. Faith is more than believing something; it is acting on what you believe. We can think and talk about doing something; but it is when we take action that we begin to see results. When these four men took action, God got involved in the equation. Sometimes we forget that miracles tend to be a combination of God and us working together. We still have to work. When those men started walking, God started working!

These four men asked a vital question: *"Why stay here until we die?"* (v.3) They took the risk of faith. As soon as they started walking, God multiplied the sound waves of their footsteps so that it sounded like a great army with horses on the march. The Arameans heard the sound and panicked. They said, *"The king of Israel has hired the Hittite and Egyptian kings to attack us!"* (v.6) The entire army fled the camp, leaving everything behind.

When the lepers arrived, they were stunned. They ate and drank and carried off the plunder and hid it. Then they realized they were being selfish. *"This is a day of good news and we are keeping it to ourselves ... Let's go at once and report this to the royal palace"* (v.9). It was a great day of celebration and deliverance for a city under siege. All because four lepers—outcasts, men who normally would not gain such easy access to the city—decided to get up and take action.

A woman once shared with me her own spiritual journey in learning to get up and take action out of depression. She battled depression often. Then she began to think about how wonderful it would be to take a short-term mission trip to get her mind off of herself and her problems and onto something else. She told me God spoke to her and said, "There's a mission field right here in Atlanta." She took that to heart and started her own missionary work. She was concerned about people suffering with AIDS. So she went to the AIDS unit at the local hospital and started to visit the patients. She encouraged them, read them Scriptures and prayed for them. She was so spiritually revived that she went back again and again. She has been renewed as she ministers to patients she describes as being open to love and desiring a relationship with God.

WE WEPT WHEN WE REMEMBERED

Sometimes depression is brought on by living in the past. This is especially true as we grow older and pass through life's stages, leaving some things behind. I often feel sadness when I remember the fun my wife and I had with our children when they were very young. But then I shake myself and focus on the times we have now.

People who delude themselves with the false notion of the "good ol' days" miss the joy of living. They tend to grow negative and cynical about the world today. But these are the best days we have—because they are the only days we have! The Hebrews in captivity were sorrowful when they remembered Zion, or Jerusalem. They thought about the city, their homes, places for community gatherings, the Temple of God and their places of business. But now it was all gone, a mere pile of rubble left in the wake of the Babylonian destruction.

While in captivity, the people relegated the glories of God to the past. They thought God was finished with them. But He had a plan for them even in Babylon. When depression strikes we tend to think that the good times are over—that we have seen our best days. But we can take heart. God sent the exiles word through a letter written by Jeremiah the prophet to give them hope that plenty of good days were ahead for them. Let it encourage your spirit.

> *This is what the* LORD *Almighty, the God of Israel, says to all those I carried into exile from Jerusalem to Babylon: "Build houses and settle down; plant gardens and eat what they produce. Marry and have sons and daughters; find wives for your sons and give your daughters in marriage, so that they too may have sons and daughters. Increase in number there; do not decrease. Also, seek the peace and prosperity of the city to which I have carried you into exile. Pray to the Lord for it, because if it prospers, you too will prosper."*
>
> Jeremiah 29:4-7

This letter gives us six practical steps to getting up from depression and taking on a new challenge. Let's look at each of these steps.

If your dream has been shattered, dream a new dream. God still has a plan for your life!

The first step is to build a new dream. If your dream has been shattered, dream a new dream. God still has a plan for your life! The Israelites were now in Babylon. They had to learn how to build a new life in exile. All their mourning over the loss of Jerusalem was pointless now. Babylon was their home, and they had to get used to it. They needed to stop surviving and start thriving!

The second step the Israelites had to take was to settle down, right where they were. Restless people need to take this counsel to heart—settle down! Develop new roots for community life. End the cycle of discontentment and restlessness. Settle down and build a life that will last. The people had to turn their attention away from Jerusalem. Yes, they wanted to be home. But they were in Babylon; while they were there, they needed to settle. Discontentment keeps us from settling down and enjoying life. Maybe you are not living where you want to be living, or you are working at a job that is less than your dream job. It is easy to grow discontented, to think that God has somehow forgotten us. But that is not what God desires, and it is not the truth. Settle down and make the best of it. Don't get caught in the trap of running from one experience to the next, looking for happiness. Settle down!

The next thing the Israelites were to do was to enjoy the fruits of their labors. God told them to *"plant vineyards and eat what they produce."* Take time to enjoy life while you're pursuing your goals. Don't get so busy being successful that you never have time to enjoy your success.

The fourth step is to focus on your family. God told the exiles to marry and have children. Family is one of the most important priorities in life. Spending time at home is the best time we spend together. Children grow up and move out so quickly. We need to enjoy their childhood while we can. Young people who are still at home need to enjoy it too. The day will come soon enough when they get on their own and have to pay all their own bills!

As all of these things are becoming part of your life, you are to live a full life. God told His people, *"Increase in number there; do not decrease."* Don't let depression diminish your life. Now is the time to enlarge and increase every area of your life. Don't become less of a person; become more of who you are capable of being.

Finally, God asked the Israelites to seek peace and prosperity for others. Live outside of yourself. Direct your prayer life toward others, not just yourself and your own issues. God told the exiles to pray for the city of Babylon. Why? Because if Babylon prospered, they would prosper. They could have been angry toward Babylon because of the exile. But what would that have accomplished? It would only have made their lives harder. We are to pray for our nation; if it prospers, we will prosper.

WE HUNG OUR HARPS ON THE POPLARS

Where I grew up, we had a big weeping willow tree in our backyard. Willows seem to express sadness, as their branches are downcast instead of pointing upward toward the sun. Depression is like that. It makes us droop over with heaviness and we hang our harps up. The harp represents praise to God—a joyful, thankful spirit regardless of our life situation. When depressed we say, "I'm going to hang it up." We hang up our dreams and goals. We can even hang up our faith. Job's wife did this when she told her husband in the midst of their calamity, *"Curse God and die!"* I encourage you to not let depression rule your life and make you hang up your praise.

The Babylonians taunted the Israelites while in captivity. *"Our captors asked us for songs, our tormentors demanded songs of joy; they said, 'Sing us one of the songs of Zion!'* " The Babylonians were saying, "We heard you Israelites singing when our army besieged Jerusalem. Let's hear you sing now that you lost the war. Where's your confidence now?" Many people sing when times are good, but lose their song in tough times. Real, authentic worship is not related to circumstances, but to God Himself. We need to put on *"a garment of praise for the spirit of heaviness"* (Isaiah 61:3, KJV).

Praise is not based on the world around us, but on the work of grace within us.

HOW CAN WE SING THE LORD'S SONG?

You can worship no matter where you are in life. Praise is not based on the world around us, but on the work of grace within us. Worship brings joy, and joy is the only antidote to depression. If you want to keep your joy, remember three promises of God. All three promises were given to the exiles during this period of history.

First, God has a plan for you. " *'For I know the plans I have for you,' declares the LORD, 'plans to prosper you and not to harm you, plans to give you hope and a future'* " (Jeremiah 29:11-13).

Second, God will make a way for you. *"See, I am doing a new thing! Now it springs up; do you not perceive it? I am making a way in the desert and streams in the wasteland"* (Isaiah 43:19).

Third, God's mercies are new every morning. *"Because of the LORD's great love we are not consumed, for his compassions never fail. They are new every morning; great is your faithfulness"* (Lamentations 3:22-23).

These principles work! What follows is a letter I received from someone who found her way out of depression and into deliverance. It is used with her permission.

> Dear Dr. Cooper,
>
> Let me start by saying thank you for preaching such a great sermon Sunday. I have to admit that initially I thought it was a "good" message and probably spoke to many people; it was not until two days later that I realized how much it spoke to me.
>
> [She then shared her background story of the previous few years of getting married and having twin girls, who at that time were five. She and her husband had to move frequently because he was in the army. This put her educational and career goals to become a physician's assistant and to work in emergency medicine on hold.]
>
> Now that my daughters are in kindergarten, I thought this would be my opportunity to go back to work and pursue my career. But every door I tried to open slammed shut in my face. I have struggled with severe depression, depression like I have never known. I went so far as to call one of the counselors from church but, ironically, she

was out of town. I pleaded with God to just show me what it is I am called to do. For five months that is all I have been doing—pleading. I haven't gotten up and started making things happen. When you encouraged us to "stop whining and start winning," it struck a chord. Through the Holy Spirit I have learned that I have been sitting around in my depression and whining, waiting for God to send me a package through FedEx with my life plan in it. I have to get up and start making things happen while listening for God's direction. I have decided to start winning.

To sum it all up, your message was my FedEx. God took me to His Word and through it showed me my life plan. That is to listen for His direction while moving ahead with my life. Thank you again for getting in our faces and preaching a message that may not make us feel good when we walk out of the church, but one that certainly makes us feel better if we apply it to our lives.

FOOD FOR THOUGHT

1. What events have triggered feelings of sadness or depression in your life?
2. What things bring you joy?
3. Review the steps for moving out of depression and into God's plan for your life. Where are you in this process? What can you do that would help you move into the next stage?
4. Write down your dreams for your life. Prayerfully ask the Lord to reveal to you His plan for your life.

4

GET A GRIP ON GUILT

In Shakespeare's play *Macbeth*, Lady Macbeth is a woman with certain ambitions for her husband. Nothing is too good for him ... not even the rule of the land. Only one thing stands in the way of her husband's ascending the throne of the kingdom: the current king. So she hatches a plot, cajoling her husband to kill the monarch. Although he does become the new king, Lady Macbeth is tortured by guilt for the role she has played in the murder. She sleepwalks and sees visions; knowing her hands have helped to shed the blood of the innocent king, she asks, "What, will these hands ne'er be clean?" Eventually, her terrible guilt leads her to commit suicide.

It makes you wonder what would have happened had Shakespeare written a wandering evangelist or pastor into his play, doesn't it?

Have you ever been tortured by the oppression of guilt? Then hear the good news: Of all that it means to be a Christian, it means first and foremost freedom from guilt through the atoning work of Jesus Christ on the cross. *"He was delivered over to death for our sins and was raised to life for our justification"* (Romans 4:25).

Guilt is a feeling of regret, remorse and shame because of something we have done that is wrong or thought was wrong, or for neglecting the good we should have done. Negatively, guilt brings on the fear of punishment, anxiety, loss of self-esteem and loneliness. Positively, guilt sets moral boundaries, leads us to repentance and motivates us to holiness. Left unresolved, however, guilt can cripple us.

Of all that it means to be a Christian, it means first and foremost freedom from guilt through the atoning work of Jesus Christ on the cross.

Guilt can be real or false. Real guilt is a result of our having broken the law of God, society's laws, or our personal code of ethics. False guilt comes from the teachings of our childhood, or it may arise from social customs that may teach us to believe some things are morally wrong when in fact they are not. As a result, we feel guilty, even though we are not actually guilty of anything. Guilt may be both objective, as in the breaking of some law or rule, and subjective, as in the resultant feeling of shame. The only way to win over false guilt is to face up to our beliefs in light of the truth. The truth will set you free!

How can we get a grip on real guilt? Confession is a first step; but with it must come repentance.

A man with a nagging secret couldn't keep it any longer. In the confessional he admitted that for years he had been stealing building supplies from the lumberyard where he worked.

"What did you take?" the priest asked.

"Enough lumber to build my own home and enough for my son's house. And houses for our two daughters. And our cottage at the lake."

"This is very serious," the priest said. "I shall have to think of a severe penance. Have you ever done a retreat?"

"No, Father, I haven't" the man replied. "But if you can get the plans, I can get the lumber!" Confession can be of no help if there is no real repentance.

Let's look at an Old Testament story. Joshua the high priest had an experience with guilt and grace that is an example for us today. Zechariah the prophet had a vision:

> *Then he showed me Joshua the high priest standing before the angel of the LORD, and Satan standing at his right side to accuse him. The LORD said to Satan, "The LORD rebuke you, Satan! The LORD, who has chosen Jerusalem, rebuke you! Is not this man a burning stick snatched from the fire?"*
>
> *Now Joshua was dressed in filthy clothes as he stood before the angel. The angel said to those who were standing before him, "Take off his filthy clothes."*

> *Then he said to Joshua, "See, I have taken away your sin, and I will put rich garments on you." Then I said, "Put a clean turban on his head." So they put a clean turban on his head and clothed him, while the angel of the LORD stood by.*
>
> Zechariah 3:1-5

Joshua, representing the people of Judah, stood before God dressed in filthy garments, which is a biblical type of sin and guilt. He felt unclean, unworthy to minister before God. How could he minister wearing dirty garments? Satan, the accuser, then appeared with Joshua before God and stood at his right side to condemn him. Satan piled on the long list of Joshua's past sins and railed at him as being unfit to serve God. Focusing on our sins, our past and our failures keeps us in a state of guilt, discouragement and depression.

HOW WE DEAL WITH GUILT

There are several ways in which we tend to deal with guilt. Left on our own, of course, there is no way we can rid ourselves of it. We are truly in need of the sacrifice Christ made for us! Let's look at some ways in which we humans try to overcome our feelings and knowledge of guilt.

The first thing many people try is denial. We attempt to simply deny the reality of our guilt. We can tell ourselves that sin is a cultural myth and that we have been programmed to feel guilty by religious stories. The secularist denies the reality of moral failure, since he thinks morality is relative. He tries to destroy the notion of God and any sense of moral absolutes so as to exonerate himself from moral obligation. The "logic" is that if God doesn't exist, then everything is permissible.

A second way we try to cope with feelings of guilt is by compensation. In this instance the legalist, like the Pharisee of old, focuses on the sins of others so he doesn't have to face his own transgressions. The legalist makes long lists of rules that fit his desired lifestyle and judges himself by them. In reality, we only need to judge ourselves by the law of love—*"Love the Lord your God with all your heart and with all your soul and with all your mind. ... love your neighbor as yourself"*—which Jesus said sums up the law and the prophets (Matthew 22:37-39).

An example of this is a young minister who took his first pastorate in the hills of Kentucky. The first Sunday he preached against the evils of horse racing. The deacons called him on Monday, explained that Kentucky is the center of horse breeding and suggested that he find some other sin to preach against. So the next Sunday he thought he'd be more understanding and preached against drinking. There was very little response from the congregation. The deacons called him that Monday and said, "Haven't you ever heard of Kentucky Bourbon? You need to preach against some other sin." The third Sunday he preached against smoking. The deacons called him on the carpet and said, "Half the congregation works in the tobacco industry. You need to preach against something else."

Finally, he asked them to choose a subject to their liking. One deacon thought for a moment and said, "Why don't you preach against the Pharisees and the Sadducees? We don't have any of them."

Another reaction to guilt is comparison: We find people worse off than ourselves and take pride in the fact that we are not like them. Jesus told the story of two men who went to the Temple to pray—one a religious leader and the other a tax collector. The religious leader prayed, *"God, I thank you I am not like all other men—robbers, evildoers, adulterers—or even like this tax collector. I fast twice a week and give a tenth of all I get."* But the tax collector was convicted of his own sin and prayed, *"God, have mercy on me, a sinner."* The religious leader compared himself with others in order to feel good about himself. The tax collector confronted the issues of his own life. Jesus said the tax collector went home justified before God, and not the religious leader. Why did He tell this story? *"To some who were confident of their own righteousness and looked down on everybody else, Jesus told this parable"* (see Luke 18:9-14).

Rationalization is a fourth way in which we try to deal with our guilt. We make excuses for our sins instead of taking responsibility for them. William Glasser, in his book *Reality Therapy,* observed, "Man is not irresponsible because he's ill; he's ill because he's irresponsible." Don't be like the man who prayed, "God, I have committed many sins, but I have several excellent excuses."

A fifth reaction is hedonism, in which we seek pleasure to overcome our feelings of guilt. We get lost in the "good life" of excess to avoid confronting spiritual issues. We drown out guilt in pleasurable experiences, substances and excessive entertainment.

Freud described the personality as having three subsystems: the Id, the Ego and the Superego. The Id is that part of our personalities that seeks to minimize pain and maximize pleasure with total disregard of the consequences. The Id is that childish part of our personalities that has to be balanced by reason (the Ego) and by conscience (the Superego).

Self-punishment is a method practiced by the religious of many types. We understand that there should be punishment, so we attempt to mete it out for ourselves, seeking self-atonement. For example, during Holy Week in the Philippines men walk down busy streets, laboring under the weight of heavy wooden crosses. They drag these along the roads, trying to find relief from their burden of sins. Young men of Pampanga mask their faces and fill the streets, beating their own backs bloody with whips. Sometimes we use guilt to punish ourselves. We ask God to forgive us, but we never forgive ourselves because we feel unworthy of mercy. But forgiveness only benefits us if we receive it.

About the year 1830, a man named George Wilson killed a government employee who caught him in the act of robbing the mails. He was tried and sentenced to be hanged. However, the President of the United States, Andrew Jackson, sent him a pardon. But Wilson did a strange thing. He refused to accept the pardon. No one seemed to know what to do. So the case was carried to the Supreme Court of the United States. Chief Justice Marshall, perhaps the greatest chief justice we have ever had, wrote the opinion. In it he said, "A pardon is a slip of paper, the value of which is determined by the acceptance of the person to be pardoned. If it is refused, it is no pardon. George Wilson must be hanged." And he was.

HOW GOD DEALS WITH OUR GUILT

The account of Joshua the high priest shows how God deals with the sin problem with the power of His forgiveness. Guilt lingers because we fail to accept the fullness of God's forgiveness. Let's look a little more closely at this account.

The Lord interceded for Joshua, saying to Satan: *"The Lord rebuke you."* Paul asked the rhetorical question, *"If God is for us, who can be against us?"* (Romans 8:31) Do you know that God is for you and not against you?

God called Himself, *"The Lord who has chosen Jerusalem."* God's calling still remained on Joshua in spite of his sin. While sin hinders our relationship to God, He does not cast us away. God never gives up on us. His gifts and callings on our lives are irrevocable—they cannot be revoked, or taken away (Romans 11:25).

God asked, *"Is not this man a burning stick snatched from the fire?"* What a graphic description of everyone who has been saved by grace! When Jesus came onto the earth, it was as though God were reaching down into this world and lifting us out of the fire of sin and judgment to give us new life. Whenever we call on God for help, He reaches down and snatches us out of the fire.

God told the angel to take off Joshua's filthy clothes. Even so, the Lord removes our sin and the record of our wrongs. *"Old things pass away; all things are become new"* (Second Corinthians 5:17, KJV). Then the angel was told to clothe the high priest in rich garments. *"For he has clothed me with garments of salvation and arrayed me in a robe of righteousness"* (Isaiah 61:10).

Whenever we call on God for help, He reaches down and snatches us out of the fire.

Jesus' classic parable of the prodigal son tells of the father who welcomed his wayward son back home. When the young man returned home destitute, the father told the servants: *"Bring the best robe and put it on him"* (Luke 15:22).

Paul tells us that we should *"Clothe yourselves with the Lord Jesus Christ"* (Romans 13:14). When Adam and Eve sinned, they needed a garment to cover their shame. God made garments for them to serve as a covering. The word *atonement*, by the way, means "to cover." What covers us as believers? *"Love covers over a multitude of sins"* (First Peter 4:8). Believers are described in the Revelation as being clothed in fine linen, which represents righteousness (Revelation 19:8).

At the cross, the only thing Jesus had left was His seamless garment, for which the soldiers gambled. There

He took our sins upon Himself. He has left us His garment of righteousness, which we wear humbly and joyfully. When you confess your sins to God, He takes away the filthy clothes of a guilty conscience and clothes you in the robe of the righteousness of Christ.

The last act in the vision of Zechariah is that of the angel putting a clean turban on Joshua's head. This is the turban of the priest. It bore the inscription, *"Holy to the Lord."* What a powerful word: *Holy*. Holiness intimidates us; it is a word fit only for God. Yet grace makes us holy. The word *holy* means "that which is set apart from the common for the uncommon, for a life dedicated to God." Moral failure makes us feel as though we are no longer worthy for service to God. Many people sit on the sideline of life feeling disqualified because of their failure. The fact is that they are forgiven, cleansed and have a calling to serve God. But guilt crushes their joy and leaves them feeling like second-class citizens. The only cure for guilt is grace. *"Where sin increased, grace increased all the more"* (Romans 5:20). Failure is never final with God!

WHAT WE NEED TO DO

Here are three action steps you need to take to get a grip on guilt:

First, admit your sins. If guilt is false, you need to realize that and free yourself from dysfunctional thinking. I have counseled people who feel guilty about being divorced even when they were the victim in the situation.

They wanted the marriage to work, but their spouse did not; yet they still entertain feelings of guilt. We need to stop feeling guilty about decisions other people make—decisions over which we have no control.

But when it comes to real guilt, we, like Joshua, have to stand before God and give an account of our actions. The Bible uses the word *repent.* Repentance means a change of mind and behavior. David prayed, *"Against you, you only have I sinned and done what is evil in your sight"* (Psalm 51:4). When David stopped covering up and started confessing, he found forgiveness. *"When I kept silent, my bones wasted away through my groaning all day long"* (Psalm 32:3). What a graphic description of the depressed feelings that come from guilt! But David took action and was honest with God. *"Then I acknowledged my sin to you and did not cover up my iniquity ... and you forgave the guilt of my sin"* (Psalm 32:5).

Second, receive by faith God's forgiveness and cleansing. When you ask God to forgive you, He does! God promises to do seven things with our sins when we admit them to Him and ask for forgiveness:

He will cover them: *"Blessed is he whose transgressions are forgiven, whose sins are covered"* (Psalm 32:1).

He removes them: *"As far as the east is from the west, so far has he removed our transgressions from us"* (Psalm 103:12).

He takes them away: *"Your guilt is taken away and your sin is atoned for"* (Isaiah 6:7).

He casts them into the sea: *"You will tread our sins underfoot and hurl all our iniquities into the depths of the sea"* (Micah 7:19).

He wipes them out: *"Repent, then, and turn to God, so that your sins may be wiped out, that times of refreshing may come from the LORD"* (Acts 3:19).

He remembers them no more: *"I will forgive their wickedness and will remember their sins no more"* (Hebrews 8:12).

He forgives them: *"If we confess our sins, he* [God] *is faithful and just and will forgive us our sins and purify us from all unrighteousness"* (First John 1:9).

The final step to getting a grip on guilt is to let go of guilty feelings. Stop using guilt to punish yourself. Some people feel guilty today about things they did or failed to do many years ago, even though they confessed long ago. They need to let it go.

In the 1550s Martin Luther fasted days without end, practiced penance and even inflicted pain on his body as he tried to punish himself for his sins. But he never found inner peace. He found freedom from guilt the day he read what Paul wrote to the Romans: *"The just shall live by faith"* (Romans 1:17, KJV). From that time on, Luther stopped trying to work his way to salvation as he trusted in Jesus Christ to save him. And he found freedom from guilt.

FOOD FOR THOUGHT

1. Is there anything that is producing feelings of guilt in your life?
2. How do you feel when you have unresolved guilt? To what can you compare your feelings and responses?
3. Look at the things you determined have been causing you guilt. According to the Scriptures, is your guilt real or false?
4. How should you resolve your guilt if it is a false guilt? What steps can you take if it is true guilt?
5. Take the steps you need to resolve your feelings of guilt. Allow the Lord to set you free!

5

GET A GRIP ON ANGER

I want to tell you a story. It seems that an elderly lady in Florida had done her shopping. Upon returning to her car, she found four young men in the act of entering the vehicle, getting ready to drive away. Furious, she dropped the groceries, drew her handgun from her purse, and screamed, "I have a gun and I know how to use it! Get out of the car!"

The four young men jumped out of the car and ran like madmen. The woman, now shaking like a leaf in the wind, picked up her groceries and got into her car. She was so shaken she could not even get her key into the ignition. She kept trying, then suddenly realized what had happened: She was in the wrong car. Her car was parked five spaces away. The woman drove to the police station and reported what had happened. The police sergeant burst into uncontrollable laughter as he pointed to four young men at the other end of the counter who had just reported a carjacking by a mad elderly woman described as white, five feet tall, with curly white hair and carrying a large handgun. No charges were filed.

How we manage anger is crucial to success in our relationships and endeavors. Anger is a fundamental part of our emotional makeup and serves a vital role in our lives, provided we keep it in check. Webster defines anger as "a feeling of sudden and strong displeasure and antagonism directed against the cause of an assumed wrong or injury; wrath; ire." It can range anywhere from mild irritation to violent fits of uncontrollable rage. Anger activates a fight-or-flight mechanism in the body which prepares us for either battle or escape. Physiologically, it releases adrenaline in the body which causes increased blood pressure, pulse and respiratory rate. Occasional bouts of anger are normal. But to live in a perpetual state of anger is detrimental both personally and interpersonally.

How we manage anger is crucial to success in our relationships and endeavors.

Anger in itself is not a sin. That's a relief! *"Be ye angry, and sin not"* (Ephesians 4:26, KJV). Or, as a more modern translation puts it, *"In your anger do not sin"* (NIV). In other words, we may be angry; but we are cautioned not to sin by expressing our anger inappropriately. Did you know that even God gets angry? In fact, of the 455 Old Testament references to anger, 375 refer to God's anger. So anger, obviously, is an appropriate response in some situations. But unresolved or uncontrolled anger is highly destructive. Studies have linked anger to high blood pressure, depression, psychological disturbances and violence, in addition to the damage done to our relationships.

Here's some solid advice about healthy, positive ways to deal with anger:

Refrain from it: *"Refrain from anger and turn from wrath; do not fret—it leads only to evil"* (Psalm 37:8).

Turn it away: *"A gentle answer turns away wrath, but a harsh word stirs up anger"* (Proverbs 15:1).

Control it: *"Better a patient man than a warrior, a man who controls his temper than one who takes a city"* (Proverbs 16:32).

Don't associate with it: *"Do not make friends with a hot-tempered man, do not associate with one easily angered, or you may learn his ways and get yourself ensnared"* (Proverbs 22:24-25).

Flee dissension: *"An angry man stirs up dissension, and a hot-tempered one commits many sins"* (Proverbs 29:22).

Cultivate patience: *"Do not be quickly provoked in your spirit, for anger resides in the lap of fools"* (Ecclesiastes 7:9).

Fear judgment: *"Anyone who is angry with his brother will be subject to judgment"* (Matthew 5:22).

> Be slow to anger: *"Everyone should be quick to listen, slow to speak and slow to become angry, for man's anger does not bring about the righteous life that God desires"* (James 1:19-20).

Although we would like to think we can handle it on our own, the only way to bring anger under control is to yield to the power of the Holy Spirit. As we live under the influence of the Spirit, we conquer the sinful nature with its ungodly expressions of anger and develop the fruit of the Spirit, which is "*love, joy, peace, patience, kindness, goodness, faithfulness, gentleness and self-control*" (Galatians 5:22, 23).

WHY WE GET ANGRY

There are several reasons why we become angry. Adam and Eve's son Cain famously committed the first murder in human history. But his rage was not directed solely toward his brother; it was rooted in his rebellion toward God (see Genesis 4:6-7). Saul breathed out murderous threats against the early Christians and gave approval to the stoning of Stephen for blasphemy (see Acts 7). Later, he met Jesus Face to face on the Damascus Road and became one of the greatest preachers of the good news of Jesus Christ the world has ever known. But his rage toward those early believers was due to his rebellion toward God by rejecting Jesus. We may not be murdering those who disagree with us, but when we get out of step with God, it negatively affects our relationships with others.

Sometimes anger can blind us to things we need to see. A priest and pastor from local churches were standing by the side of the road during a heavy rain pounding a sign into the ground that read: "The End Is Near! Turn yourself around before it's too late!" A man went speeding by and yelled, "Leave us alone, you religious nuts!" From around the curve they heard the screeching of tires, followed by a big splash. The pastor said to the priest, "Do you think the sign should just read, 'Bridge Out'?"

There are several reasons people grow angry. Let's look at some of the causes, then see how we can get a grip on anger.

Perhaps the most prevalent reason for anger is immaturity and self-centeredness. When we can't get what we want, we may act out in anger. Some people simply never outgrow temper tantrums.

Jealousy and insecurity are other common causes of anger. We feel that our position or security are threatened, and we get angry. King Saul was jealous of David's favor with the people and his growing popularity. His jealously turned to such rage that David had to flee the court of Saul when Saul threatened to kill him.

A third factor, not surprisingly, is stress. Highly stressed people experience anger when they feel trapped by circumstances beyond their control. In fact, those who suffer from chronic hostility may be at risk of heart disease.

Unfinished business is another frequent indicator. The most powerful form of unfinished business is deep-seated resentment from the past. In the Old Testament we read that the nation of Edom *"harbored an ancient hostility"* against Israel (Ezekiel 35:5). The conflict in the Middle East is based on many ancient hostilities, as are other conflicts between nations. Many people harbor ancient hostilities that go back generations in their families. If you want to get a grip on anger, you have to travel light and throw off the excess baggage of resentment.

If you want to get a grip on anger, you have to travel light and throw off the excess baggage of resentment.

Another common cause of anger is controlling behavior. Perfectionists or people with an obsessive-compulsive disorder often get angry because they cannot control people or circumstances. They try everything in their power to manipulate people by fear, guilt or threats. They are constantly telling God how to run the universe because they can't trust Him to do all things well. And they become angry when things don't turn out as they had planned, hoped, prayed or expected.

A final cause of anger is injustice. There is a time for anger. On one occasion the Gospels record that *"Jesus looked ... at them in anger"* (Mark 3:5). Jesus drove money changers out of the temple in a fit of holy rage because of their extortion in the house of God. You see, anger can motivate us to take social action. Rosa Parks, who recently passed away, has been honored by our nation for her act of heroism the day she refused to give up her seat on a bus and move to the back of the bus. She was angry—in a quiet, calm and reserved fashion. She was angry enough not to take injustice any longer. Her courageous act was a pivotal moment in fueling the Civil Rights Movement, which gave freedom and equality to the oppressed.

HOW NOT TO DEAL WITH ANGER

Let's look at some common, yet ineffective, ways of dealing with anger.

Disguise is probably familiar: Peace at any price; don't rock the boat. The extreme case is the martyr complex by which we absorb all injustices, deserved and undeserved, without an appropriate response. We confuse this response with turning the other cheek. Anger can be disguised, hidden behind the masks of silence, cynicism or such passive-aggressive behaviors as pouting, stubbornness, gossip, procrastination and argumentativeness.

Sometimes we push painful memories or thoughts from the level of conscious awareness to an unconscious level through denial. This is called repression. We do this because the memories are so painful or traumatic that we don't know how to deal with them. Or perhaps we just can't confront the reality of what has happened to us.

We try to convince ourselves we aren't angry at people or God or life, while all the time the anger is eating away at us. But anger is like energy: It cannot be destroyed, only stored or altered to another form. Repressed anger troubles the mind, affects our relationships and produces health problems such as ulcers, headaches and high blood pressure if left unresolved. This is why the Scripture says, *"Do not let the sun go down while you are still angry"* (Ephesians 4:26). We need to confront the issues that make us feel angry and learn to express that anger in a way that is healthy and beneficial.

A third ineffective means of dealing with anger is by explosion. You'll recognize this reaction if you've seen it! Some people express their anger destructively by reactions of rage. They allow their anger to build until they explode. They may knock a hole in the wall, throw an object, kick the dog, blast you with profanity or resort to physical abuse. Today our society advocates venting our anger. But anger must be expressed within proper limits.

HOW CAN WE MANAGE ANGER?

Let's go to Jesus' anger management seminar, delivered during the Sermon on the Mount.

Step one: Cultivate the spirit of the peacemaker:

> *"Blessed are the peacemakers, for they will be called sons of God."*
>
> Matthew 5:9

We all want to live the good life. So let's remember Peter's steps to the good life:

> *Whoever would love life and see good days must keep his tongue from evil and his lips from deceitful speech. He must turn from evil and do good; he*

must seek peace and pursue it.

First Peter 3:10-11

Nowhere does God say in His Word, "Blessed are the troublemakers."

Step two: Go and be reconciled:

"Therefore, if you are offering your gift at the altar and there remember that your brother has something against you, leave your gift there in front of the altar. First go and be reconciled to your brother; then come and offer your gift."

Matthew 5:23-24

To *reconcile* means to restore peace in a broken relationship. As a peacemaker, it is our part to make the first step toward reconciliation.

Step three: Settle matters quickly:

"Settle matters quickly with your adversary who is taking you to court. Do it while you are still with him on the way, or he may hand you over to the judge, and the judge may hand you over to the officer, and you may be thrown into prison. I tell you the truth, you will not get out until you have paid the last penny."

Matthew 5:25-26

Don't let relational issues go unresolved. Settle matters of dispute and disagreement quickly, and do not allow any root of bitterness to grow in your life.

Step four: Turn the other cheek:

> *"You have heard that it was said, 'Eye for eye, and tooth for tooth.' But I tell you, Do not resist an evil person. If someone strikes you on the right cheek, turn to him the other also."*
>
> Matthew 5:38-39

This does not mean that we are to submit to abusive behavior. Rather, it means we are to act independently of others' actions toward us. Don't react to anger with anger. Choose your response. Remember, *"A gentle answer turns away wrath"* (Proverbs 15:1).

Step five: Don't throw your pearls to pigs:

> *"Do not give dogs what is sacred; do not throw your pearls to pigs. If you do, they may trample them under their feet, and then turn and tear you to pieces."*
>
> Matthew 7:6

Jesus is saying that we should never tell someone something they are not ready to hear. If we do, they may turn on us and tear us to pieces with their words. Confrontation can be risky business. When we confront someone, we need to make sure we chose the right manner in which to speak to the person, the right time to address the subject, and the proper setting so that he or she has time and space to process our confrontation.

Let's get to the bottom line in getting a grip on anger. Paul wrote, *"I will show you the most excellent way"*

(First Corinthians 12:31). That way is love. The Christian life is the most excellent way to live.

> *Love is patient, love is kind. It does not envy, it does not boast, it is not proud. It is not rude, it is not self-seeking, it is not easily angered, it keeps no record of wrongs. Love does not delight in evil but rejoices with the truth. It always protects, always trusts, always hopes, always perseveres. Love never fails.*
>
> First Corinthians 13:4-8

In December of 1983, Pope John Paul II entered a cell at Rebibbia Prison outside Rome. He met with inmate Mehmet Ali Agca, the man who had fired a bullet at his heart. In a private moment together, Pope John Paul forgave his would-be assassin. His life in the Word had taught him the value of peacemaking; his walk with God had given him the grace to walk in reconciliation.

FOOD FOR THOUGHT

1. Think about how you handle anger. What triggers your anger? What causes it to dissipate?
2. What are the ways in which you deal with anger? How do these line up with the Scriptures?
3. How might you respond if someone expresses anger toward you? What if you have done nothing wrong?

6

GET A GRIP ON CIRCUMSTANCES

The only survivor of a shipwreck washed up on a small, uninhabited island. He prayed to God to save him, and every day he scanned the horizon for help; but no one came. Finally, he built a hut and put his few possessions into it. One day, after hunting for food, he arrived back to find the hut in flames, the smoke rolling up to the sky. He was angry and frustrated as a sense of hopelessness washed over him. But early the next day, a rescue ship arrived. "How did you know I was here?" he asked the captain.

"We saw your smoke signal," the captain replied.

This is an example of divine providence. *Providence* is a way of saying that God watches over us to provide and to protect. Paul puts it this way: *"In all things God works for the good of those who love him, who have been called according to his purpose"* (Romans 8:28).

This is one of the most powerful, yet most often misunderstood, statements in the entire Bible.

This passage both comforts and challenges us. The phrase *"all things"* is not limited to adversities, but also includes blessings. This statement is too often interpreted to refer to life's difficulties; but God works in all things. He is the source of every good and perfect gift. When you get an unexpected blessing, pause and ask, "How is God working in this situation?" When adversity comes, ask, "How is God working?" Seek to live a God-centered life.

When people do not understand the ways of God, they may become alarmed over their circumstances, not realizing that God's hand is in all things. For instance, there were three men sitting in the waiting room of a hospital. A nurse walked over to the first and said, "Congratulations! You're the father of twins!"

"What a coincidence," he replied. "I work for the Twin City Federal."

A while later, the nurse came out to congratulate the second man. "You're the proud father of triplets!" she told him. "That's funny," he responded. "I work for AAA." At that, the third expectant father jumped up, a look of terror on his face, and ran out of the room.

"Where are you going?" the nurse called out.

He yelled over his shoulder, "I work for 10,000 Auto Parts!"

GOD DOES NOT CAUSE ALL THINGS

People tend to misunderstand the statement, *"All things...work together for good to them that love God ..."*

(Romans 8:28, KJV) Does this mean God causes all things? No. It means that God works in all things. He is at work in everything. I have come to a new understanding and appreciation of this Scripture: "[God] *works out everything in conformity to the purpose of his will*" (Ephesians 1:11). Let the implication of that truth settle in your mind.

God's foreknowledge is not causative, but God works in all things. He allows history to unfold on its own and only intervenes to ensure that His eternal purpose is fulfilled. The fact that God knows all things does not mean He causes all things. He has given us the freedom to act, and we experience both the good and the bad consequences of our decisions.

It is our decision, ultimately, that determines whether we operate within or outside of the boundaries of God's will.

You see, human freedom has limits. Man has freedom of will only within the larger boundaries of God's will. The Creator endowed man with free moral agency and warned him of the catastrophes caused by sin as well as the incredible blessings produced by obedience. It is our decision, ultimately, that determines whether we operate within or outside of the boundaries of God's will.

Because God is sovereign, He ultimately rules over the final outcome of human history. But we must understand that He does not cause every single event. God's sovereignty is the boundary within which we exercise the freedom of our will. We can never do anything that will ultimately thwart the purpose of God for our world. We may limit His purpose and blessings in our life, but God's larger purpose for the world will stand until the end of time.

Christians are like teabags. You never know what's in them until you put them into hot water!

When Abraham Lincoln was assassinated, most of this country went into mourning. There was confusion, despair and hopelessness. In New York City, a crowd gathered and was expressing their dismay at the loss of their great leader and their concern about the future. Suddenly a man climbed up the stairs of a building where he could look over the crowd and shouted with a loud voice:

"The Lord reigns over Washington!"

The people grew silent as the meaning of his words reassured them. Slowly they began to disperse and go about their business.[12]

CIRCUMSTANCES ALONE DO NOT SHAPE CHARACTER

President John F. Kennedy in his book, *Profiles in Courage,* wrote, "Great crises produce great men and great deeds of courage." This sounds true, but it is not quite accurate.

Circumstances do not produce character; they reveal character. They tend to bring out what is already within us. I once read that Christians are like teabags. You never know what's in them until you put them into hot water!

The choice is ours. It is what we do with our circumstances that makes us or breaks us. Lord Acton famously said, "Power tends to corrupt, and absolute power corrupts absolutely." But power alone does not corrupt us. It's what we do with it and how we handle fame and position that matters. Wealth does not change a person. It's what that person does with it that counts. Adversity does not destroy people; it is how they handle it that determines the ultimate outcome. When someone says we need trouble to develop us or that God is sending trouble in order to teach us something, know that those things are not true. Adversity ruins as many people as it refines. People can become bitter or better through adversity. It all depends on how they handle it.

Perspective is power. Psychologist Albert Ellis developed a counseling model called Rational Emotive Therapy.[13] I've outlined it below:

A	+	B	=	C
ACTIVATING EXPERIENCE		BELIEF SYSTEM		EMOTIONAL CONSEQUENCE

In his model, *A* stands for the *activating experience* (what happens to us), *B* stands for our *belief system* (how we interpret the problem), and *C* stands for our *emotional consequence* (how we feel). According to Ellis, it is a faulty assumption to believe that *A* (what happens to us) causes *C* (how we feel). The intervening variable is *B*—our perception, interpretation or belief about what happens to us. The circumstances of life do not determine our level of emotional suffering or our happiness; rather, what we believe about what happens to us ultimately determines how we feel. Feeling is subject to thinking.

Here's a formula to remember whenever tough times come your way:

PROBLEM + PERCEPTION = PAIN OR PEACE

We make the choice between victory and defeat by the way we react to the situations of life. That's good news! We are in control of our emotional state and not mere victims of whatever happens to us.

Corrie Ten Boom, survivor of Hitler's death camps, learned how to tap into the triumphant power of faith. In her autobiography *Tramp for the Lord,* she shares this anonymous poem that helps us put life's adversities into perspective:

My life is but a weaving, between my God and me.
I do not choose the colors He worketh steadily.
Oftimes He weaveth sorrow, and I in foolish pride,
Forget He sees the upper, and I the underside.
Not till the loom is silent, and shuttles cease to fly,
Will God unroll the canvas and explain the reason why.

The dark threads are as needful in the skillful Weaver's hand,

As the threads of gold and silver in the pattern He has planned.[14]

A few years ago I sat spellbound as I listened via radio to a Chinese pastor who had been imprisoned for his faith. While in prison he witnessed for Christ to the other prisoners and to the prison guards. Many of them accepted Christ as their Savior. So his captors sought to silence him by placing him in solitary confinement. He was forbidden a Bible, not allowed to pray or to sing, and was shut off from the other prisoners to prevent him from preaching.

In addition, he was assigned the job of working the cesspool. Alone. The first day he stepped into the cesspool and the door slammed shut behind him, he realized quickly how blessed he was. Since no one could hear him, he could pray and sing as loud and as long as he wanted. Month after month he enjoyed rich fellowship with God in the cesspool.

He said his favorite song to sing in the cesspool was the hymn, "In the Garden." As this man of God reflected on his years in prison, he began to recite the first verse over the radio airwaves:

I come to the garden alone while the dew is still on the roses,

And the voice I hear falling on my ear, the Son of God discloses.

And He walks with me, and He talks with me,
And He tells me I am His own;
And the joy we share as we tarry there,
None other has ever known.[15]

Then he said to the interviewer, "I survived those years alone in prison because I learned to turn a cesspool into a garden."

Whatever stress, loss or difficulty you face in life, you too can turn the cesspool into a garden and know beyond a shadow of a doubt: *In all things God works for your good.*

GOD PROVIDES GRACE, BUT NOT ALWAYS AN EXPLANATION

Let's think about circumstances, conditions and consequences. We have a tendency to lump all life events into the same category. There are connecting points between circumstances, conditions and consequences. Some things happen to us, while other experiences are the direct result of our choices, good and bad, or the choices of others which affect us. We reap the consequences of what we sow, both positively and negatively. When you are experiencing something in life you don't understand, stop and ask, "Is this experience a circumstance over which I have no control, a condition of some decision, or a consequence of some action?"

Question God's ways, but not His character. The entire Book of Habakkuk consists of a series of episodes of the prophet asking God, "Why?" as he pondered the plight of his people. In the end, he found grace and hope, writing, *"Yet I will rejoice in the LORD, I will be joyful in God my Savior"* (Habakkuk 3:18). Job was a man who did not have an answer from God to explain his suffering, pain and disappointment; but he received the grace to help him get through it. Job came out better, not bitter, because he trusted God. Paul the apostle wrote of his struggle over what he called *"a thorn in my flesh."* God didn't remove it, but He gave Paul grace to endure it. With newfound understanding, Paul could write, *"When I am weak, then I am strong"* (Second Corinthians 12:10).

Question God's ways, but not His character.

Are you in a difficult situation? Does there appear to be no way out? Then know that the way out may be the way through. The way out of your adversity may be the long, arduous way of going through it. We always want God to snatch us out of our problems, but sometimes He has a different plan. To get out of Egypt and enter into the Promised Land, you have to go through the wilderness. David wrote of walking through *"the valley of the shadow of death"* (Psalm 23:4). He knew he wasn't there to stay; he was passing through. We prefer that God would keep us out of the valley in the first place, or snatch us out rather than lead us through. We must remember, however, that God does lead us through the valley. He never leaves us in it! I like Paul's thinking on this matter: *"God is faithful ... When you are tempted, he will also provide a way so that you can stand up under it"* (First Corinthians 10:13). The way of escape is actually the power to endure what you are facing. God will give you grace, power and joy to face any challenge and to be victorious.

GOD USES ALL THINGS FOR OUR GOOD

I like the fact that God works in all things *"for our good."* God never works for our harm, only for our good. A cartoon strip of Dennis the Menace shows Dennis and his friend Joey leaving Mrs. Wilson's house with their hands full of cookies. Joey says to Dennis, "I wonder what we did to deserve this?"

Dennis says, "Look, Joey, Mrs. Wilson didn't give us cookies because we're nice. She gave them to us because she's nice." So it is with God.

God, the Artist and Builder, finishes what He starts. He uses every experience to complete His purpose for us. The psalmist wrote, *"The LORD will fulfill his purpose for me"* (Psalm 138:8). Paul echoed this thought in his letter to the Philippians: *"Being confident of this, that he who began a good work in you will carry it on to completion until the day of Christ Jesus"* (Philippians 1:6).

Michelangelo described his sculpting work as "the making of men." He approached the process of sculpting as freeing men from the prison of stone. Instead of trying to fashion the image of a man from stone, he envisioned himself merely chiseling away the excess stone around the already existing image within. He could look at the raw stone and see David, the *Pieta*, Moses, and the

Bacchus. Sometimes he quit in frustration. He left his statue of Matthew half finished, explaining that the stone refused the release the prisoner. He left several works unfinished, four of the most famous being the *Captive Giants* in Florence. But our God is an Artist Who always finishes His work!

How will you use your circumstances? Someone said to me recently, "I wonder how God will use this experience for His glory?"

I replied, "The real question is, 'How will you use the experience for God's glory?' "

FOOD FOR THOUGHT

1. In what circumstances does God work for good in the lives of those who love Him? (See Romans 8:28.)
2. Do you see Him at work in your circumstances? In what situations in your life right now is it more difficult to see His hand and caring?
3. What can you do to help yourself get a grip on those circumstances?

7

GET A GRIP ON CHANGE

If you could change one thing about your life, what would it be? How we manage and broker change is a major key to our success. We live in a world of continual transition. For some, change is alarming, threatening the *status quo*. For others, it is exhilarating, filling life with adventure.

Change comes in two forms: that over which we have no control, and that which we ourselves initiate. Change in itself is not constructive. It must be developmental and growth-oriented in order to be of benefit to us. For instance, moving furniture around is not developmental change; it's merely a change in arrangement. You still have the same furniture. You can rearrange the clothes in your closet, but that doesn't give you a new wardrobe. We can make all kinds of cosmetic changes, but they aren't substantial changes with lasting importance.

Paul Harvey told the story of a man who said, "I grew up poor; but they told me I wasn't poor, I was needy. Then they told me I wasn't needy, I was deprived. Then they told me I wasn't deprived, I was underprivileged. Then they told me I wasn't underprivileged, I was disadvantaged. I still don't have a dime, but I have a great vocabulary."

I read recently, "When you're through changing, you're through." Organizational change can be highly emotional for everyone involved. Jeanie Daniel Duck, in *The Change Monster*, observes, "When people—executives, in particular—start a change initiative, they believe they understand what will be involved. But, once they get into the process, they are always astonished at how muddled, painful, protracted, tiresome, complicated, and energy-consuming creating change can be."[16] It is the human part of the equation that these executives miss—they are bringing change into the lives of others, and they do not foresee the resistance they will meet in the process.

Jesus told a parable to illustrate the importance of managing change. His entrance into the world marked a new day—the kingdom of God had come in a new and dynamic way. It came like a seed which is planted and grows over time to become an expansive tree. Many religious leaders of the day cherished the old ways and could not adjust their thinking to the new ideas of Jesus. They were rigid in their thinking and could not accept Christ's new concepts. He challenged them to open themselves to what God was doing using two metaphors.

> *"No one sews a patch of unshrunk cloth on an old garment. If he does, the new piece will pull away from the old, making the tear worse. And no one pours new wine into old wineskins. If he does, the wine will burst the skins, and both the wine and the wineskins will be ruined. No, he pours new wine into new wineskins."*
>
> Mark 2:21-22

"No one puts a new patch on an old garment." The new patch had not yet shrunk. When it got wet it would shrink and tear away from the old garment. There comes a time when we can no longer patch things up and renovate. We need to discard the old and get something new. Quit sewing up the garment and get yourself a new pair of pants!

"No one pours new wine into old wineskins." Wineskins of that era were made from animal skins. Over a period of time they would become hard and brittle. Eventually they would break. In Jesus' parable, the wine is the grace of God. The old wineskins were the traditions of the law. The new wine would burst the old wineskins, because the wineskins couldn't stretch—just as some people are rigid in their thinking. They have God in a box. But God will not stay in a box! Because of their unyielding mindset, the religious leaders of Christ's day missed what God was doing in their time. Jesus said to them, *"You did not recognize the time of God's coming to you"* (Luke 19:44).

Luke's account of the parable of the wineskin adds Jesus' saying, *"No one after drinking old wine wants the new, for he says, 'The old is better'* " (Luke 5:39). He meant that some people are reluctant to change. They are stuck in the past and tend to like what they are accustomed to. They don't even taste the new wine. They fail to give it a chance. The truth is that over time, as the new wine seasons, it will become the best wine of all.

...reaching your goals is a marathon, not a sprint—so pace yourself.

Let's look at five steps of productive change and transformation to help you become the person God made you to be and to reach your highest potential: You must set your course, change your mindset, set realistic goals, enjoy the journey, and get up when you fail.[17]

SET A COURSE

Change for the sake of change is unwise. Productive change is based on having set a course, but also on making necessary adjustments in the process. All goals need to be revised at times, and the strategy for reaching goals reviewed. Financial planners teach people to rebalance their portfolio yearly, because the markets change. Remember, reaching your goals is a marathon, not a sprint—so pace yourself. All major decisions boil down to two questions that must be answered:

First, where do you want to go? Decide the direction for your life. Possess a vision of what you want to accomplish.

Second, how do you plan to get there? This question deals with developing a strategy and the objectives necessary to reach your goals.

CHANGE YOUR MINDSET

The Gospels record 38 parables of Jesus. What's a parable? It is an earthly story with a heavenly meaning. The purpose of Christ's parables was to change the way people thought, especially about the kingdom of God. Paul exhorted believers to *"Be transformed by the renewing of your mind"* (Romans 12:2). Before we can change, we need to understand why the change is important. The mind has to accept the pros and cons of change. You have to believe it! Losing weight, or saving money, or managing time is achieved only after you believe it is important to do so. Thought is followed by desire. You have to want to make the change. Things won't change just because someone advocates it. You have to believe it for yourself.

Leon Martel, in *Mastering Change,* describes three common traps that keep us from recognizing and using change.

The first trap is believing that yesterday's solutions will solve today's problems. I once heard Robert Kiyosaki, author of *Rich Dad, Poor Dad,* speak. He said that the most important principle for gaining wealth is to change the way people think about wealth. He pointed out that the idea of getting a job and working there for life so you can retire is a concept based on the industrial age. However, we live in the information age. In the industrial age, the longer a person worked for a company, the more valuable he was and the more he was worth. In the information age, the longer a person works, the less valuable he is to the company.

The second snare is assuming that present trends will continue. I enjoyed Greek mythology in high school. I liked learning about the myths and legends of other cultures. But I would not try to live my life believing in these tales. People tend to develop all sorts of cultural and historical myths that keep them locked into unproductive ways of living. It is truth that sets us free.

The third trap that can keep us from embracing change is neglecting the opportunities offered by future change. When either our fear of change or the desire to maintain the *status quo* keeps us from growing, we forfeit future opportunities.

SET REALISTIC GOALS

Lasting change happens incrementally and slowly over time. The brain has to get used to the idea of change so the body can adapt. The same is true of organizations. You have to develop a strategy to navigate your way through change. In his book *Transitions,* William Bridges, who researched various professionals experiencing major life changes, noted that every significant change possesses three essential stages: Endings, The Neutral Zone, and The New Beginning.[18]

Endings are actually beginnings! An ending, in this sense, is the beginning point of change. It involves a grief process that takes us through the steps from denial to resistance to acceptance. Coming to terms with the finality of the old in order to dream of the new is the most painful aspect of endings.

The Neutral Zone is a period of reorientation, an in-between time characterized by uncertainty and instability. People between jobs, parents whose last child has left home for college, individuals who have retired but not yet developed a retirement lifestyle, or churches whose long-term pastor has retired all serve as examples of the Neutral Zone. However, this period should be a time to celebrate the past without impulsively rushing into the future. New ideas and directions need to be explored before action is taken. The Neutral Zone is merely the winter between green and growth.

In the New Beginning, hope is rekindled and new vision imparted. A renewal of the original purpose or establishment of a new purpose for the individual, family or organization births a new beginning. Hold to God's promise found in Jeremiah 29:11: *"I know the plans I have for you...plans to prosper you and not to harm you; plans to give you a hope and future."*

ENJOY THE JOURNEY

I think one of the often overlooked aspects of Jesus' personality is His sense of joy and humor. Despite all the responsibilities He carried, He enjoyed life. One of the last things He said to His followers conveyed this: *"I have told you this so that my joy may be in you and that your joy may be complete"* (John 15:11). He was facing the cross, yet He spoke of His joy.

Enjoy the benefits of change. The Christian life is a process, as John Bunyan described it in his classic work, *Pilgrim's Progress.* I meet so many people who want to know everything about the Bible; but it is the process of learning and discovering that brings joy to life. You have to enjoy the benefits of the change, or that change won't last. Monitor your changes so you can see progress, which will encourage you to stay the course. If you can, get the support of others who celebrate your success.

When I was a boy, our family took a vacation trip to Miami. I remember it: Loading seven people into a station wagon with no air conditioning. Stopping for a lunch of tomato sandwiches wrapped in waxed paper, eaten under a tree. Hanging over the front seat, begging my father to answer the deepest question in my mind at that point in my life: "Are we almost there?" That's not a vacation—it's purgatory! There's a reason man invented airplanes! But we get so focused on getting there in so many pursuits of life that it's hard to enjoy the journey. We keep asking God, "Are we there yet?" And He answers, "Enjoy the journey!"

The process is as important as the destination, for it is a goal in itself. I have had to learn this through our church's recent building campaign. On one hand, I was anxious to get through; on the other, I found joy in watching how the Lord used the process to develop us individually and as a body of believers. The process of construction made us better disciples, more committed to the kingdom, and more of a community with a common mission.

Lasting change and growth take time. Rome wasn't built in a day, nor should it have been. Process is vital, as Jesus affirmed in the parable of the sower. In Matthew 13 we read of Christ's teaching; of the sower going out and planting in four kinds of earth, of what happened as the new plants grew or shriveled, thrived or fell. The seed that sprouted quickly also perished quickly because it had no root. It takes time to grow roots. If things—people, marriages, organizations, businesses—grow too quickly without a good root system, they are uprooted and destroyed during a storm.

GET UP WHEN YOU FAIL

One of my favorite passages is Micah 7:8: *"Do not gloat over me, my enemy! Though I have fallen, I will rise!"* Don't overreact to failure and mistakes, making them out to be the end of the world. The apostle James, the half-brother of Jesus, said that we need to confess our faults to each other so that we can be healed (James 5:16).

Setbacks are to be used to recommit to goals and to get back on track. One of the most touching stories in the Gospels is Christ's encounter with Peter after the resurrection. He called him the second time by the Sea of Galilee. He never mentioned Peter's failure, but appealed to him on the basis of love.

"Peter, do you love Me?" asked Jesus.

"Yes, Lord, You know that I love You," he replied.

Jesus then gave him a new commission: "Feed My sheep."

Peter used his failure—his denial of Jesus—as a springboard to launch himself to a new level as a more dedicated disciple of Jesus and a world changer.

FOOD FOR THOUGHT

1. Describe the differences between developmental change and a change in arrangement. Assess several areas of change in your life right now. Which type of change are they? Which type is easier for you to deal with?
2. What are the five steps of productive change and transformation? Choose one area of change in your life—either one with which you are currently involved or something that you would like to change. How can you use these five steps to help you in making this change?
3. What are three traps that can keep us from embracing change?

8

GET A GRIP ON PRIORITIES

A group of friends went deer hunting and paired off for the day. That night one of the hunters returned alone, staggering under the weight of an eight-point buck. "Where's Harry?" the others asked.

"Harry had a stroke of some kind. He's a couple of miles back up the trail."

"You left Harry lying there, and carried the deer back?"

"Well," said the hunter, "I figured no one was going to steal Harry."

Real success and significance in life is based on well-established priorities. A priority is that which is of first importance. We need to identify our priorities and then commit to them with discipline.

God used circumstances to force King Hezekiah to reexamine his priorities in life. The Lord sent the prophet Isaiah to the godly King Hezekiah with a troubling message:

"Get your house in order, you are going to die" (see Second Kings 20:1).

Establishing priorities is like a spring cleaning for the soul and spirit.

Knowing that we are facing our eternal destination gives us a sense of destiny. Hezekiah was very ill, at the point of death. His mind was preoccupied with reflections on his life and on what impact he had made. We too want to make an impact. We need to live with heaven in view (see Psalm 90:12, Matthew 6:19-21, Second Corinthians 5:10, Colossians 3:1, Hebrews 9:27). Isaiah's message was about priorities. Let's break the statement down: *Get your house in order.*

ORDER REQUIRES ORGANIZATION

"Get your house in order." The words *order* and *priority* are interchangeable. We have to keep things in their proper place. It takes intentionality, planning and work to get things in order. Establishing priorities is like a spring cleaning for the soul and spirit. God put us here to rule and to maintain order (Genesis 1:28). Our greatest challenge is to rule ourselves. Why bother? Because law gives order (Romans 13:1). Freedom is not found in anarchy. As Thomas Jefferson said, "The price of freedom is eternal vigilance."

However, becoming organized isn't the most important part of establishing priorities; we can be organized and still not do what needs to be done.

A man cut his hand and went to the hospital. He went through the emergency room doors and found himself in a hallway with two doors. One was marked *Men* and the other, *Women*. He went through the one for men and found himself in a hallway facing two more doors: *Over 55* and *Under 55*. He walked through the one for the younger men and found two more doors: *Injury above the Belt* and *Injury below the Belt*. He went through the appropriate door, only to find himself facing yet two more doors, marked *Injury External* and *Injury Internal*. Proceeding through the door marked *Injury External*, he saw two more doors: *Injury Major* and *Injury Minor*. He went through the door for minor injuries and found himself back in the parking lot. As he got back into the car his wife asked, "Did you get any help?"

"No," he replied. "But they were very well organized."

ORDER INVOLVES IMPORTANCE

Some things are more important than others. These are sometimes designated as being "first." For instance, the gospel is of first importance (First Corinthians 15:3). We are to seek first the kingdom of God (Matthew 6:33). We are to offer the first fruits in our giving—not the leftovers (Proverbs 3:9). We must evaluate our goals, responsibilities, relationships and commitments and ask ourselves which are most important. Determining priorities involves not only distinguishing between the important and the unimportant, but also between the important and the most important.

Surprised to see an empty seat at the Super Bowl stadium, a diehard fan remarked about it to a woman sitting nearby. "It was my husband's," the woman explained. "But he died."

"I'm very sorry," said the man. "Yet I'm really surprised that another relative or friend didn't jump at the chance to take the seat reserved for him." "Beats me," she said. "They all insisted on going to the funeral."

ORDER MEANS TIMING AND SEQUENCE

I believe it was Pascal who said, "The thing one knows is what to put first." First things first. Don't get the cart before the horse. Or, in our vernacular, don't put the U-Haul before the SUV! Do things at the proper time and in proper sequence. As the Scriptures say, *"There is a time for everything, and a season for every activity under heaven"* (Ecclesiastes 3:1). God moves in seasons to perform His will. This is why we cannot hurry God in His work. People get things out of sequence. For example, couples live together to see if they want to be married. Yet sociology reveals that couples who do live together before wedlock are more likely to get divorced.

This issue is important with money management. We get confused about our goals: retirement, insurance, personal savings, college funds for our children. Some of these need to be established first.

The story of Haggai reveals a time when the kingdom of God was not first in importance for the people of

Israel. Their lack of spiritual priorities caused things not to work out well in their lives.

> *This is what the LORD Almighty says: "These people say, 'The time has not yet come for the Lord's house to be built.' " Then the word of the LORD came through the prophet Haggai: "Is it a time for you to be living in your paneled houses, while this house remains a ruin?" Now this is what the LORD Almighty says: "Give careful thought to your ways. You have planted much, but have harvested little. You eat, but never have enough. You drink, but never have your fill. You put on clothes, but are not warm. You earn wages, only to put them in a purse with holes in it."*
>
> Haggai 1:2-5

Was the problem a lack of wealth, time or knowledge? Not at all. It was a lack of proper priorities.

ORDER MEANS PEACE

God has established order in the things He has made. We see this first in the seven days of creation. The sun governs the day and the moon, the night. We are made in His image, complete with creative ability. And we are to create a world of order, not chaos. Righteousness, doing things properly according to God's Word, brings peace and harmony (Isaiah 32:17, 48:18; James 3:18). Jesus said, *"Seek first his kingdom ... and his righteousness"* (Matthew 6:33).

The Bible addresses the principle of order and peace on many issues: Times and seasons are orderly (Genesis 8:22); Satan is the author of chaos (Second Corinthians 4:4); God is the Author of order and peace in worship (First Corinthians 14:33, 40); self-centeredness brings chaos (James 3:16); and obedience brings a well-ordered life (Deuteronomy 28:3-9).

ORDER MEANS BALANCE

There are several areas of our lives which are of equal importance. For example, my relationship with God is important, but my relationship with my wife is equally important. Even Jesus connected two commandments as one—love God and love your neighbor. In other words, both are of equal importance. Work is important, but rest is equally important so that I remain healthy.

Let's bake a priority pie. Imagine a pie with each piece representing an important area of your life. Priority living does not mean that you must sacrifice one for the other. It means maintaining balance so that each piece of the pie receives its proper due. All priorities cannot be listed in order of importance. Many share equal importance. Priorities are like slices of a pie, each with its appropriate place. There are four main slices to the pie. The first is faith, which includes worship, communion with God, and discipleship. The second piece is work; this section is comprised of a career and financial stewardship. The third slice is love, for family and friends; this bit of pie includes romantic love as well. The last slab of pie is play—recreation, leisure, hobbies and entertainment.

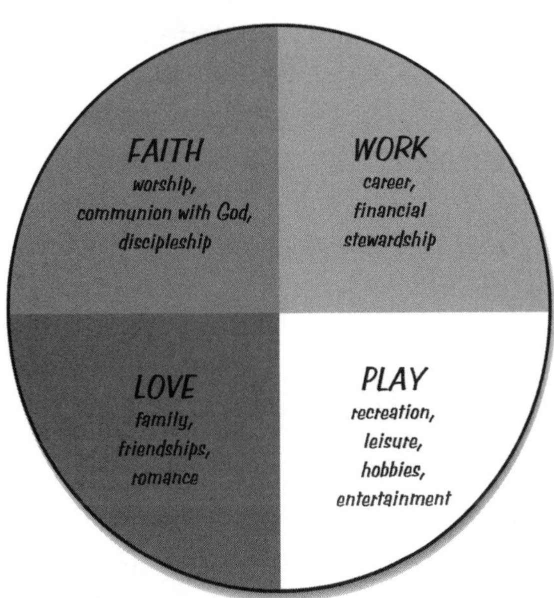

In her book *A Practical Guide to Prayer*, Dorothy Haskins tells about a noted concert violinist who was asked the secret of her mastery of the instrument. The woman answered the question with two words: "Planned neglect." Then she explained. "There were many things that used to demand my time. When I went to my room after breakfast, I made my bed, straightened the room, dusted, and did whatever seemed necessary. When I finished my work, I turned to my violin practice. That system prevented me from accomplishing what I should on the violin. So I reversed things. I deliberately planned to neglect everything else until my practice period was complete. And that program of planned neglect is the secret of my success."

Jesus tells us that the thread which runs throughout every priority in our lives is the kingdom of God. So the essential question of the disciple is this: "Does every area of my life serve the interests of the kingdom of

God?" David Livingstone, missionary to Africa, said, "I will place no value on anything I have or may possess except in relation to the kingdom of Christ."

So the essential question of the disciple is this: "Does every area of my life serve the interests of the kingdom of God?"

Over the triple doorways of the Cathedral of Milan there are three inscriptions spanning the splendid arches. Over one side arch is carved a lovely wreath of roses. Under the flowers are the words, "All that which pleases is but for a moment." Over the other side arch is a cross, with the inscription, "All that which troubles us is but for a moment." But at the great central entrance to the main aisle are the words, "That only is important which is eternal."

FOOD FOR THOUGHT

1. List the things in life that are priorities for you. How do they fit into the "priority pie" of faith, work, love and play? Do you see a balance of priorities?
2. What areas of your life currently need to be put in order? How do these areas fall into the priorities you have already established?
3. Is there an area in which "planned neglect" might be helpful in your life, to enable you to focus on your real priorities?

9

GET A GRIP ON WORRY

A dense fog that covers a seven city-block area one hundred feet deep is composed of less than one glass of water divided into 60,000 million drops. Not much is there, but it can cripple an entire city. So it is with worry. Worry cripples our dreams and aspirations, leaving us paralyzed by fear.

I was standing in Starbucks waiting for a hot chocolate when my drink was called: "Dr. David." A woman standing nearby asked, "Who are you?" I said, "David Cooper. I am a minister in Atlanta." Somewhat desperately she said, tears welling in her eyes, "Would you please pray for me? I was fired from my job. I am really struggling with anxiety." I was able to speak briefly with her about trusting the Lord whose name is Jehovah Jireh, the Lord our Provider.

What is worry? It is an anxious or fearful state of mind that can cause increased muscle tension, upset stomach, anxiety and depression. Chronic worriers often suffer from low self-esteem. The Greek word for worry means "to be inwardly divided or distracted;" the English word comes from an Anglo-Saxon word meaning "to choke or strangle." Put simply, worry is a mind vacillating between doubt and faith. E. Stanley Jones said, "Worry is the sand in the machinery of life." I like this modern beatitude: "Blessed is the man who is too busy to worry during the day, and too sleepy to worry at night." Often our worry or anxiety can lead to wrong decisions.

...worry is a mind vacillating between doubt and faith.

For instance, Joe and Dave were out deer hunting when suddenly Dave keeled over dead. Frantic, Joe called 911 on his cell phone and blurted," My friend has just dropped dead! What should I do?"

A soothing voice at the other end said, "Don't worry, I can help. First, let's make sure he's really dead."

After a brief silence the operator heard a gunshot ring out. Then Joe came back to the phone.

"Okay," he said nervously to the operator. "What do I do next?"

Here is Jesus' counsel on getting a grip on worry:

"So my counsel is: Don't worry about things—food, drink, and clothes. For you already have life and a body—and they are far more important than what to eat and wear. Look at the birds! They

don't worry about what to eat—they don't need to sow or reap or store up food—for your heavenly Father feeds them. And you are far more valuable to him than they are. Will all your worries add a single moment to your life?

"And why worry about your clothes? Look at the field lilies! They don't worry about theirs. Yet King Solomon in all his glory was not clothed as beautifully as they. And if God cares so wonderfully for flowers that are here today and gone tomorrow, won't he more surely care for you, O men of little faith?

"So don't worry at all about having enough food and clothing. Why be like the heathen? For they take pride in all these things and are deeply concerned about them. But your heavenly Father already knows perfectly well that you need them, and he will give them to you if you give him first place in your life and live as he wants you to.

"So don't be anxious about tomorrow. God will take care of your tomorrow too. Live one day at a time."

Matthew 6:25-34, TLB

LEARN FROM NATURE

Jesus' first step in handling worry is to learn from nature. *"Look at the birds of the air and the lilies of the field,"* he said. Deism states that God created the world but has left to us to our own devices. Deism is Bette

Midler singing, "God is watching us from a distance." But Jesus taught that God is ever near, as close as a breath of wind.

Creation reveals the providence of God. He cares for and watches over His creation. Jesus said, *"Are not two sparrows sold for a penny? Yet not one of them will fall to the ground apart from the will of your Father. And even the very hairs of your head are all numbered. So don't be afraid; you are worth more than many sparrows"* (Matthew 10:29-31).

How much is one billion? Start counting now and you'll die before you reach the number. Now, there are 100 billion stars in our galaxy, the Milky Way. If you start now, it will take you 3,000 years to count to 100 billion. Yet God has numbered the stars and calls them all by name. *"He ... brings out the starry host one by one, and calls them each by name"* (Isaiah 40:26). God is mindful of everything you are experiencing, and He cares for you. David sang of God's providence: *"How precious to me are your thoughts, O God! How vast is the sum of them! Were I to count them, they would outnumber the grains of sand. When I awake, I am still with you"* (Psalm 139:17-18). David realized that he was in the thoughts of God 24/7! And so are we.

So, *"cast all your anxiety on him because he cares for you"* (First Peter 5:7). Anxiety asks, "What if?" What if you fail? What if you go bankrupt? What if you can't finish what you started? What if you get sick? What if...? Anxiety and worry haunt us with the *what ifs* of life.

Faith is the only answer to anxiety and worry. Abraham was tested by God; God asked that he take his son Isaac, whom he loved, to Mount Moriah to become a sacrifice. What a time of testing! When they went up the mountain and were preparing to worship, Isaac asked Abraham, "Father, where is the lamb?" They had everything they needed for the sacrifice except the lamb. Abraham answered simply, "God will provide." Those three words are the only response we need to battle worry. "God will provide." (See Genesis 22:1-14.)

Fear can be defined as *F*alse *E*xpectations *A*ppearing *R*eal. President Roosevelt wisely quoted Winston Churchill in his inaugural address, given in the wake of the Great Depression: "The only thing we have to fear is fear itself."

Here's how you can fight worry:

> *Do not be anxious about anything, but in everything, by prayer and petition, with thanksgiving, present your requests to God. And the peace of God, which transcends all understanding, will guard your hearts and your minds in Christ Jesus.*
>
> Philippians 4:6-7

A French soldier in World War I used to carry this writing to help him overcome worry:

> Of two things, one is certain. Either you are at the front, or you are behind the lines. If you are at the front, of two things, one is certain. Either you are exposed to danger or you are in a safe place. If you are exposed to danger, of two things one is certain. Either you are wounded or you are not

wounded. If you are wounded, of two things one is certain. Either you recover, or you die. If you recover, there is no need to worry. If you die, you cannot worry. So why worry?

The God of Providence...

... covered Adam and Eve with skins of atonement after they sinned.

... gave Cain a second chance after he murdered his brother.

... called Abraham to a land he would receive as his inheritance.

... provided a substitutionary sacrifice on Moriah.

... exalted Joseph to the throne of Egypt.

... sent Moses to Egypt on a mission of mercy.

... parted the Red Sea.

... kept Israel in the wilderness.

... provided a land flowing with milk and honey.

... took a shepherd boy from the field to the throne.

... sustained Elijah during a famine.

... kept Daniel in the lion's den.

... walked through the fire with the three Hebrew children.

... took five loaves and fed a multitude.

... placed a cross on Golgotha's hill and redeemed humanity.

... rose triumphant on the third day.

... sent the Holy Spirit as our Comforter and Guide.

... preserved the writing and transmission of Scripture.

... provided a place for us in heaven with Him.

... has secured the future when the King of kings returns in triumph.

God is able to do exceeding abundantly above all we ask or think!

LET GO OF CONTROL

Jesus asks a provocative question: *"Will all your worry add a single hour to your life?"* Worry can't add hours to our lives, but it can certainly take them away. So control what you can control and leave the rest to God. Recognize the limitations of worry.

Worry is an exercise in futility. It won't pay the bills, secure a job promotion, restore a marriage, control your children, heal sickness or make you happy. An average person's anxiety is focused this way: 40 percent on things that will never happen; 30 percent on things about the past that cannot be changed; 12 percent on things that have been criticized by others, mostly untrue; 10 percent about health, which gets worse with stress; and 8 percent about real problems that will be faced.

Worry is a luxury no one can afford. Anxiety is a contributing factor in high blood pressure, arthritis, heart disease and ulcers. *"Be careful,"* Jesus cautioned, *"or your hearts will be weighed down with dissipation, drunkenness and the anxieties of life"* (Luke 21:34).

Worry is a luxury no one can afford.

Worry is contrary to faith. *"We live by faith, not by sight"* (Second Corinthians 5:7). But God honors faith. *"Without faith it is impossible to please God, because anyone who comes to him must believe that he exists and that he rewards those who earnestly seek him"* (Hebrews 11:6).

I believe it was Hudson Taylor, one of the earliest missionaries to China, who gave this excellent advice to those who were accepting the challenge of missionary work: "Let us give up our work, our plans, ourselves, our lives, our loved ones, our influence, our all, right into [God's] hand; and then, when we have given all over to Him, there will be nothing left for us to be troubled about."

LEAN ON GOD FOR PROVISIONS

"The pagans run after all these things," Jesus said in reference to material provisions (Matthew 6:32). They are consumed with the material and are unconcerned with the spiritual. Our view of eternity changes our sense of significance. A current TV reality show is entitled *Fight for Fame.* Unfortunately, young people are being taught to pursue fame. What young people need is spiritual purpose, not temporary fame.

Where is your citizenship? Our ultimate citizenship is not in an earthly kingdom but in the kingdom of God. *"Our citizenship is in heaven"* (Philippians 3:20). When we take our place in the kingdom and our eternal inheritance in heaven seriously, it changes the way we relate to life.

We live in a time of materialism. Yet the material passes away. It is the eternal that lasts forever. We need to trust God to provide for us and we need to focus more on spiritual matters. Jesus put it this way:

> *"Do not store up for yourselves treasures on earth, where moth and rust destroy, and where thieves break in and steal. But store up for yourselves treasures in heaven, where moth and rust do not destroy, and where thieves do not break in and steal. For where your treasure is, there your heart will be also."*
>
> Matthew 6:19-21

Many people today are savvy about investing. Making sound financial investments is important. But when it comes to money, we have to consider how we are spending, saving and investing our wealth for the advancement of the kingdom of God.

Jesus is not telling us not to save and invest money. He clearly taught the importance of financial investment for economic growth in His parables. But making money and accumulating wealth does not make us successful, for wealth is not the measure of significance. How many people have achieved fame, fortune, power and pleasure but led empty, meaningless lives? It is only when we invest our lives in the advancement of the kingdom of God and live for a higher purpose that we attain eternal significance.

When we seek first the kingdom, God provides us with all we need. You won't need to worry about your provisions again when you get your priorities in order and put the kingdom of God first. When you do, God will take care of the rest. You will discover what Abraham discovered—God will provide!

FOOD FOR THOUGHT

1. God is Jehovah Jireh, our Provider. What kinds of things has He provided for you in your life? What times of special provision or blessing do you recall?
2. Is there currently a need in your life that has not yet been met?
3. Ask the Lord to help you to abstain from worry, giving every situation over to Him. If you listed a concern above, take time now to pray over it. Ask God if there is anything you should be doing about it; then trust it to His care.

10

GET A GRIP ON DECISIONS

Today we hear a lot of talk about destiny. Despite popular belief, destiny is not predetermined; it is decided by the choices we make. You don't discover your destiny, for that implies a pre-scripted life; rather, you decide it. God created you with the freedom of choice.

The first words God spoke to Adam when He created him and put him in the Garden of Eden were, *"You are free"* (Genesis 2:16). Everyone needs to hear God say that to them. You are not the victim of the decisions of others, even though you have been adversely affected by them. Even though your current circumstances may not be what you want, you are now free to decide what you want to do with your life.

God created us with purpose. He has a plan for each of us, but it is not a detailed script. God has not mapped out every detail of your life. That is for you to decide. You are God-created but self-molded. God has given us talents and potential, and He expects us to use what He has invested in us.

When people think their destiny is already predetermined, it can have a negative effect on them. First, they are paralyzed by the fear of making the wrong decision. They also spend much of their time searching (with no success, I might add) for secret, hidden keys to discovering the mysterious will of God which always seems to elude them. They function under the false belief that discovering their destiny will guarantee them success.

...destiny is the sum total of a person's decisions over the course of his life.

Destiny is not predetermined. Rather, destiny is the sum total of a person's decisions over the course of his life. It is determined by every significant decision you make. This knowledge of what destiny really is will empower you to take charge of your life and enable you to reach your highest potential.

We need to learn to make good decisions if we are to reach our potential. God promises us direction. The Scriptures are filled with assurances of God's plan and help in this area. Moses sang, *"In your unfailing love you will lead the people you have redeemed. In your strength you will guide them to your holy dwelling"* (Exodus 15:13). God promised: *"I will instruct you and teach you in the way you should go; I will counsel you and watch over you"* (Psalm 32:8). Asaph prayed, *"You guide me with your counsel, and afterward you will take me into glory"* (Psalm 73:24). *"The steps of a good man are ordered by the LORD"* (Psalm 37:23, KJV). *"Your ears will hear a voice behind you, saying, 'This is the way; walk in it' "* (Isaiah 30:21). Jesus promised the Holy Spirit *"will guide you into all truth"* (John 16:13). And Paul wrote: *"For those who are led by the Spirit of God are sons of God"* (Romans 8:14).

God's guidance may not always be as loud and clear as we would like. I heard of a lady who was walking down the street one day. She heard a voice yell, "Stop! If you take one more step, you'll be killed!"

She halted in her tracks. Seconds later a brick fell from a building right in front of her. A minute or two later she started to cross the street when the same voice bellowed, "Halt! Don't cross the street now!"

Suddenly a truck sped by; it never even slowed as it ran the red light. Shaken, the woman asked, "Who are you?"

The voice replied, "I'm your guardian angel. I imagine you have some questions for me."

"I sure do," the woman responded. "Where were you on my wedding day?"

Here is the best counsel I know of for making wise decisions: *"Trust in the LORD with all your heart and lean not on your own understanding; in all your ways acknowledge him, and he will make your paths straight"* (Proverbs 3:5-6).

TRUST IN THE LORD

Expect God to guide you if you are seeking His will. Hearing God's voice is a natural experience, not something strange. It is logical that God would speak to us, since prayer is a conversation with God. How does God speak to us? His voice may sound like words in our minds. Since God created us with the power of language, is it only common sense to expect Him to communicate to us in ways we can understand.

Should we expect God to bring us His Word through an old man with a long white beard, looking like a character from *The Lord of the Rings*? Perhaps he would carry an ancient leather scroll, sealed with seven seals, with a word from God for our lives? No; God speaks in the mind.

Here are three practical steps to tuning in to God's voice.

Prayer: Ask God for wisdom, and listen to the inner voice of the Holy Spirit. Here's a great promise: *"If any of you lacks wisdom, he should ask God, who gives generously to all without finding fault, and it will be given to him"* (James 1:5).

Industrialist Robert G. LeTourneau, manufacturer of earth-moving equipment, received a wartime order from the government to develop a machine to lift airplanes. No such machine had ever been conceived, much less built. LeTourneau and his engineers went to work on the problem. They were baffled. Frustration set in as every think-tank meeting came up empty. One day, as evening approached, the team was feverishly at work when LeTourneau got up from the meeting and said, "I'm leaving to go to the prayer meeting at my church."

"Prayer meeting?" they exclaimed. "You can't do that. We've got a deadline to meet!"

"But I've got a deadline with God," he replied. He went on to the prayer meeting. Forgetting his problems, he entered into singing with the congregation and prayed with others about their needs. On his way home, while walking down the street, he reported that suddenly the full design of the machine appeared in his mind, complete with every detail.

Partnership: Seek the counsel of wise and experienced friends, leaders and mentors. We become like the company we keep. We are cautioned not to associate with the wrong counsel. *"Oh, the joys of those who do not follow evil men's advice, who do not hang around with sinners, scoffing at the things of God"* (Psalm 1:1, TLB). Good advice is crucial for good decisions. *"For lack of guidance a nation falls, but many advisers make victory sure"* (Proverbs 11:14). This is one of my favorite proverbs: *"He who walks with the wise grows wise, but a companion of fools suffers harm"* (Proverbs 13:20).

Peace: Only make a decision when you are at peace. Peace is the final decision-maker. If you don't have peace in your decision and you don't know what to do, do not act prematurely. Wait for the peace of God to rule in your heart. This is not to say that you still won't have some anxiety about a major decision. That's to be expected. But overriding all anxiety is the confidence that you are making the right decision. *"Let the peace of Christ rule in your hearts"* (Colossians 3:15)

LEAN NOT ON YOUR OWN UNDERSTANDING

Trust in the LORD with all your heart and lean not on your own understanding; in all your ways acknowledge him, and he will make your paths straight.

Proverbs 3:5-6

This Scripture may be confusing to some. Shouldn't we think about our decisions? Yes, we should. The passage does not mean that we should not use reason, for God Himself gave us the power of reason. Faith is logical. One of the names given to Jesus is the *Word of God. "In the beginning was the Word"* (John 1:1). The Word is *logos* in the Greek language, meaning "logic." Following Jesus as Lord is the most logical way to live!

But there are times God leads us in ways that may not at first seem logical. In fact, sometimes God's leading may seem to be contrary to logic. There are times when God's ways make absolutely no sense to us. Nevertheless, when we know God is directing our ways, we are to trust Him and not be limited by our own understanding. God sees the big picture. He sees the end from the beginning. We can trust Him. But our vision is limited. We can only see the immediate, the things that lie just before us. God reminds us:

"This plan of mine is not what you would work out, neither are my thoughts the same as yours!

For just as the heavens are higher than the earth, so are my ways higher than yours, and my thoughts than yours."

Isaiah 55:8-9, TLB

Do you remember the account of God's calling of Abraham? God called him to leave his home and go to the unfamiliar land of Canaan. Abram obeyed the Lord and went, even though he didn't know where he was going (Hebrews 11:8). He knew the general direction, but he had to take the first step and trust God to lead him in the next step. God only told him to leave. *"The LORD had said to Abram, 'Leave your country, your people and your father's household and go to the land I will show you' "* (Genesis 12:1).

Just one word—*leave!* Now here's the clincher: *"Even though he did not know where he was going!"* Abram went on an adventure with God. When he obeyed the first instruction by leaving his homeland, God showed him the next step. But He did not reveal it until Abram had taken the first step by faith. God doesn't always show us what lies around the next corner. He expects us to take the first step before He shows us the next one. This is what it means to walk by faith and not by sight. Sometimes we don't understand why God is telling us to do something. Sometimes we only have one word from God. But when you act on that one word, God will show you the next step. God's will unfolds one step at a time in a great adventure. As humans, we want a guarantee before we take that first step. We want to know how everything will turn out. But God doesn't work that way. He never takes the adventure out of life. God Himself is the guarantee. He doesn't give a guarantee—He is the guarantee! And His word to us never fails. When God speaks, even though you may not understand it with your finite mind and thoughts, don't lean on your own understanding. Trust Him and act on His word, for His word never fails.

We have to take the step of faith. *"The steps of good men are directed by the Lord. He delights in each step they take. If they fall it isn't fatal, for the Lord holds them with his hand"* (Psalm 37:23-24, TLB). But you have to give God something to guide. You can't sit idly by, waiting for God's will. Notice that this Psalm tells us that God directs our steps. Unless we are taking steps, there's nothing for God to direct.

Many people want to know the future. But God wants us to walk by faith and to trust Him with the things to come. He unfolds His plan for us little by little, one step at a time. Have you ever watched a movie a second time? You already know what's going to happen next. The adventure is gone. I recently took Barbie to a movie that I had already seen. At every suspenseful scene she would whisper, "What's going to happen next?"

I said, "Watch the movie!"

We ask God, "What's going to happen next in my life?"

God says, "Watch the movie! Enjoy the adventure of your life!"

Sometimes we are paralyzed by fear, yet say we are waiting on God. But the fact may be that He is waiting for us to take a step. Waiting on God is no substitute for taking positive action.

An older couple went to a restaurant and was told there would be a wait of about an hour. "Young man, we're ninety years old," the man told the host. "We may not have an hour." They were seated immediately. Positive action works!

IN ALL YOUR WAYS ACKNOWLEDGE HIM

What happens when we acknowledge God first in all we do? *"He will direct your paths."* You can also translate that phrase, *"He will make your paths straight."*

God's direction does not mean manipulation. Many people feel as though they are pawns on a cosmic chessboard in a match between God and the devil. But we have the power of choice. We are free, responsible and accountable for our choices. You have complete freedom to decide how you want to live.

God's direction may involve several good options. Everything in life is not predetermined, with a right or wrong decision. This confuses some people, because they think there can be only one right choice for every decision. You may have several good job opportunities, for example, and any one of them will be a good choice. God indeed directs and provides, but that does not always mean there is some mystical predetermined will of God for every decision we face.

God's direction often happens in ways of which we are not aware. God *"works out everything in conformity with the purpose of his will"* (Ephesians 1:11). This is why we need to trust Him to guide us and not lean on the limitations of our understanding. We can all look back over the course of our lives and see how God guided, protected and provided when at the time we couldn't see the hand of God. Looking back at our past reveals the unseen hand of God. It is always easier to see how God has worked when we are past an experience than it is to find His direction in the midst of a crisis.

The psalmist describes this truth: *"Your path led through the sea, your way through the mighty waters, though your footprints were not seen"* (Psalm 77:19). God leads us through the sea and the waters as He led the Israelites through the Red Sea. We may not see His footprints, but we may rest assured that God is with us. Max Lucado once wrote, "When you can't trace God's hand, trust His heart."

If we seek to follow God's direction, we submit our plans to His purposes. *"Many are the plans in a man's heart, but it is the LORD's purpose that prevails"* (Proverbs 19:21). We need to make plans and develop strategies, but we must bring them to the altar of the Lord and submit them to His purpose.

God's direction for our lives is not just a series of isolated decisions. We cannot ask God for direction for a particular decision and then fail to surrender the totality of our lives to him. We are to acknowledge Him *in all our ways*—not in some of our ways or in the ways that are convenient, but in every area of life. Paul the apostle prayed that *"Christ may dwell in your hearts through faith"* (Ephesians 3:17). To *dwell* is to take up permanent residence. May Christ be at home in our hearts, reigning as Lord over the totality of our lives!

In a Berlin art gallery is a painting by German painter Adolf von Menzel (1815-1905) which is not quite finished. King Frederick the Great is artistically portrayed speaking with his generals. In the center of the painting is a section etched in charcoal outline indicating the artist's intention to paint the king. But the artist died before the painting was finished. He had painted the background and the generals first, but the king he left till last. This work of art is the contribution of a man who omitted the king.

Don't leave God out of your thoughts, plans, marriage, relationships, business, ministry, finances, education or family. Keep God at the center of all you are and all you do. Seek to honor Him in every facet of your life.

And He will direct your paths!

FOOD FOR THOUGHT

1. Have there been times in your life when you could not see God in your circumstances, but now you can look back and see the footprints of God? (Psalm 77:19)
2. If you are facing a decision now, think about what you can do to begin to walk out your destiny in this matter. How can you start to walk so that God may direct your steps?
3. Describe what destiny means to you. What things do you envision as being part of your destiny?

11

GET A GRIP ON TIME

H.G. Wells' classic science fiction novel *The Time Machine* (1895) explores the question of whether it is possible for man to travel through time. The story deals with a man who wants to travel back in time to save his fiancé from a tragic death. Unable to do so, he travels into the future, seeking to know how to manipulate time—only to discover that he cannot.

Some wish they could travel back in time in order to correct the past. Others wish they could travel into the future to understand the course of human history. The truth is that we are all traveling through time en route to eternity.

God gave us the system of time in creation as a means of organizing life. Genesis records that the Creation took place over the course of seven days. Every day God deposits into our lives 24 hours, or 1,440 minutes, or 86,400 seconds. Time can be invested, wasted, used or neglected, but it cannot be saved. Time exists in the realm of eternity and will one day give way to the timeless when God makes a new heaven and a new earth.

Perhaps success in this life has more to do with time management than anything else. Love takes time. Financial investing takes time. Building a business takes time. Getting an education takes time. Building a church takes time. Raising kids takes time. God teaches us to use our time wisely.

The most important aspect of the stewardship of life is the stewardship of time. *"There is a time for everything, and a season for every activity under heaven"* (Ecclesiastes 3:1). *"Whoever obeys his command will come to no harm, and the wise heart will know the proper time and procedure. For there is a proper time and procedure for every matter"* (Ecclesiastes 8:5-6).

Jesus lived His life with an incredible sense of time. He said, *"Yet a time is coming and has now come when the true worshipers will worship the Father in spirit and truth, for they are the kind of worshipers the Father seeks"* (John 4:23). He prayed, *"Father, the time has come. Glorify your Son, that your Son may glorify you"* (John 17:1).

The Scriptures contain much solid advice for time management. *"Be very careful, then, how you live—not as unwise but as wise, making the most of every opportunity, because the days are evil"* (Ephesians 5:16).

Be sure you recall our look at priorities, though. You don't want to focus your management on the small things alone and crowd out the more important matters. A businessman I heard of had that problem. He was taking a seminar on time management and had completed a case study of his wife's routine for fixing breakfast. He presented the results to the class.

"After a few days of observation, I quickly determined the practices that were robbing my wife of precious time and energy," he reported. "Taking note of how many trips she made from the kitchen to the dining room carrying just one item, I suggested that in the future she carry several items at a time."

"Did it work?" the teacher asked.

"It sure did," replied the businessman. "Instead of taking her 20 minutes to fix my breakfast, it now takes me just seven."

So, how are we to travel through time?

MAKE PEACE WITH YOUR PAST

The past is a rich resource for us. We draw from history. Bible history is a source of faith. Our personal history gives us a sense of connectedness. The past influences us in ways of which we are not aware. But the past can also be a hindrance to the present.

We need to let go of the transgressions of the past. Each day is a fresh gift from God; His mercies are new every morning (see Lamentations 3:23-24). I often pray the prayer of David in the morning: *"Let the morning bring me word of your unfailing love"* (Psalm 143:8). Sometimes it is good to make a list of our sins, then picture ourselves walking up to Calvary and nailing it to the cross of Christ (Colossians 2:13-14).

The trials of the past can also hinder the present. Trials come in many shapes, forms and fashions—divorce, marriage and family stress, the death of a loved one, financial pressure, sickness, bankruptcy, and failure. Trouble is no respecter of persons. Jesus reminded us, *"In this world you will have trouble"* (John 16:33). God doesn't waste any experience, and neither should we. So *"consider it pure joy ... whenever you face trials of many kinds"* (James 1:2).

We also need to let go of the triumphs of the past. We can be so caught up in polishing our trophies that we fail to set new goals. Yesterday's trophies need to motivate us today to accomplish new goals. Don't let your life become a museum where you display the trophies of the past.

Someone once asked Rembrandt, "Of all your paintings, which one is the greatest?"

"I don't know," he replied. "I haven't painted it yet."

There is yet more to experience. There are more victories to know, more struggles to overcome, more troubles to yield to the Lord. There are more trophies to win.

One day Charles Schwab received a telegram from one of his salesman telling him that he had just sold the largest single order for steel in the history of the company. Mr. Schwab received the telegram the next day and wired back, "That's wonderful. What have you done today?"

MAKE THE MOST OF THE MOMENT

There's an interesting statement in the Bible which I find very motivational: *"Today, if you hear his* [God's] *voice, do not harden your hearts"* (Hebrews 4:7). What is God saying to you today? Are you hardening your heart by fear, doubt or small-mindedness? Or are you tuned to His voice and ready to act promptly as He leads?

Every day is a new opportunity. Today is all you have. Time stops for no one. When Queen Elizabeth was dying she said, "I would give all my possessions for one more moment of time."

The problem is procrastination. The word comes from two Latin words, *pro* meaning "forward" and *cras*, meaning "tomorrow." We procrastinate because we fear failure, or to rebel against authority, or simply because we haven't learned how to manage our time. As Mark Twain said, "Never put off until tomorrow what you can put off until the day after tomorrow."

Celebrate this day! Receive this day with thanksgiving. It's the only day we have. Begin every day by declaring, *"This is the day the LORD has made; let us rejoice and be glad in it"* (Psalm 118:24). Complaining seems to come so easily. But we are taught to *"do everything without complaining or arguing"* (Philippians

2:14). I don't know of anyone who has mastered this yet, but it is a goal to shoot for. Regardless of how difficult some days may be, we need to celebrate and decide to be thankful. One Thanksgiving Day I reflected on all the things of life for which am I am thankful, or should be thankful, and wrote a modern psalm.

I WILL GIVE THANKS

I will give thanks in all things, for God works in all things; and God works for the good of those who love Him and who are called according to His purpose. There are no coincidences, only divine opportunities.

I will give thanks for all things, for things pleasant and for things painful. In pleasant times I experience the heights of happiness; in painful times I learn to trust God.

I will give thanks for overlooked blessings ... the kind word, the encouraging letter, the daily provisions I tend to take for granted, the opportunity to work and to be productive, the common routines of every ordinary day.

I will give thanks for my family; for my wife, who is my constant companion; for my son, who brings joy to my heart; for my daughter, who fills my life with gladness; for my parents, whose love is undying.

I will give thanks for my friends; those who care enough to tell me the truth; those who love enough to make sure I have everything I need; those who believe in me through life's ups and downs.

I will give thanks for the hassles of life: a demanding schedule, traffic jams, personal responsibilities, meaningless tasks, inspiring challenges, interruptions, the alarm clock when it ends the perfect dream, cell phones that keep me continually on call ... all these remind me of the sacred privilege of being alive.

I will give thanks for the Word of God ... a lamp unto my feet and a light unto my path, a sure Word in an age of confusion, a timely Word in seasons of pain, a reassuring Word in the prison of fear, a healing Word for the wounds of the soul.

I will give thanks for America; for the cost of freedom; the promise of opportunity; the courage of patriotism; the sacrifice of warriors; the glory of the Constitution; and a government of the people, by the people and for the people.

I will give thanks for this day, for it is the gift of God. It is the only day I have, a day filled with endless opportunities and bright promises. And I shall get everything I can from it and give everything I have to it.

I will give thanks to the Lord, for He is good; His love endures forever.

Consecrate this day. Joshua challenged Israel's leaders to this end: *"Choose for yourselves this day whom you will serve."* Then he declared his own commitment: *"As for me and my household, we will serve the LORD"* (Joshua 24:15). Make it your life's ambition to glorify God. Decide to do something every day to honor the Lord and to build the kingdom of God. It may be by praying for others, encouraging someone, or showing kindness in His name.

Make it your life's ambition to glorify God. Decide to do something every day to honor the Lord and to build the kingdom of God.

Conquer this day. You may fight a battle today. Face it with a warrior's mindset, determined to win. You will be a victor and not a victim. You will live larger than life. Some people say, "I dread this day." But we are to conquer the day and its challenges instead of being defeated by it.

Jesus said, *"In the world ye will have tribulation: but be of good cheer"* (John 16:33, KJV). This was not just some sort of pep talk for the disciples; it was instruction for life. Jesus did not speak these words lightly; indeed, when He uttered them, He was facing the cross.

When life hurts, when disappointments come, when things don't turn out as you had planned, rise above it.

Declare confidently, *"I can do everything through him* [Christ] *who gives me strength"* (Philippians 4:13).

One summer evening during a violent thunderstorm, a mother was tucking her small boy into bed. She was about to turn off the light when he asked with a tremor in his voice, "Mom, will you sleep with me tonight?"

The mother smiled and gave him a reassuring hug. "I can't, dear," she said. "I need to sleep with Daddy."

A long silence was broken at last by his shaky little voice: "That big sissy."

Capitalize on this day. Don't waste a moment, but take full advantage of the day. Don't waste today by regretting the past or by sitting around like a couch potato. Dream your dreams, use your gifts and work hard to make this day the best day of your life.

After Michelangelo died someone found in his studio a piece of paper on which he had written a note to his apprentice: "Draw, Antonio, draw, and do not waste time."

Colonel Harland Sanders was sitting on his porch in Shelbyville, Kentucky, on his 65th birthday when the mailman came up the walk and handed him his first social security check. While grateful, he had no intention of settling down and retiring from business. He decided to use his modest check to launch a new career. He came up with an idea—and ideas are powerful. He reflected on the delicious fried chicken his mother used to make, crispy brown and tender. He could almost smell the aroma of the chicken cooking as he sat on his porch. He came up with the idea of selling his mother's recipe on a royalty basis to restaurant owners. He took action immediately, driving in his battered car to every restaurant owner he could find, telling them about the special recipe, but no one was interested.

He went all the way to Utah to sell his idea. Finally, a restaurant owner there was impressed by Colonel Sander's enthusiasm and decided to give it a try. The result was an over-crowded restaurant serving golden brown chicken marketed with the motto Sanders coined: "It's finger lickin' good." Sanders sold out his interests for $2 million and then was hired by the new owners as goodwill ambassador at an annual salary of $40,000. Such is the power of creative enthusiasm.[19]

MAKE PREPARATIONS FOR YOUR FUTURE

While we don't need to waste time and energy worrying about tomorrow, we should make preparations for it. Scripture teaches that children should not have to save up for their parents, but parents for their children (Second Corinthians 12:14). We should also prepare for eternity. We are eternal beings who live in a world of time.

My daughter Charlsi and I walked to the top of Kennesaw Mountain when she was very small. When we got to the top we sat down on the granite rocks among the Civil War canon mounts overlooking Atlanta. Engraved in a granite stone was a Bible verse: *"Prepare to meet thy God"* (Amos 4:12, KJV). Charlsi slowly read the words out loud. Then she looked up at me and asked, "Does that mean God was here?"

I replied, "Well, sort of."

Jesus said, *"No one can see the kingdom of God unless he is born again"* (John 3:3). That's how you get ready for eternity.

Getting a grip on time boils down to knowing what is most important and devoting our time to it instead of allowing the tyranny of the urgent and the crushing demand of every emergency to eat away at our time until we have little of it left to enjoy.

FOOD FOR THOUGHT

1. What kinds of things make demands on your time? Think about your priorities. Do the things you spend time on match up with your priorities in life?

2. Are there things you can do each day to bring honor to the Lord and to further His kingdom? What are they?

3. Have you made peace with your past? If so, offer a prayer of thanks. If not, pray and ask the Lord to help you in this area. Ask forgiveness where that may be needed; pray a blessing on those who may have hurt you; pray for those whom you may have hurt. Ask the Lord if there is any action you should take to make things right again.

12

GET A GRIP ON PERFECTIONISM

The title of a new movie caught my attention—*The Perfect Man*. It's the story of a widow and her daughter. In it, the mother meets a man who is the perfect husband and father. My mind went back to a couple in premarital counseling who had asked me, "Are marriages made in heaven?"

I responded, "Yes, but the maintenance work takes place on earth."

Let's talk about getting a grip on perfectionism. Perfectionism is the measuring of one's worth on the basis of a flawless performance. What I do, then, tells me who I am. The perfectionist may be a workaholic, or the nice guy who always tries to please everyone, or the martyr who makes limitless sacrifices. Perfectionism is a pitfall which leads to guilt, depression, a negative self-image, frustration in relationships and burnout in our work. The goal of perfectionism is affirmation. Perfectionism is rooted in the lack of love and self-acceptance. It begins in our childhood as we perform for love.

There is a difference, yet a fine line, between perfectionism and excellence. God calls us to excel: *"Whatever your hand finds to do, do it with all your might"* (Ecclesiastes 9:10). *"Whatever you do, work with all your heart, as working for the Lord, not for men"* (Colossians 3:23).

Perfectionists have many positive traits. Their goal-directedness, attention to detail, and persistence in working for success results in tremendous achievements. But the drawbacks are their inability to relax or to cope with failure, and their relentless pursuit of a level of perfection which can never be achieved. In fact, perfectionism does not increase one's efficiency, but rather hinders it. In one study of 150 salespeople, 40 percent of whom were deemed perfectionists, the researchers found differences in the perceived quality of life between perfectionists and non-perfectionists. The former felt they were under greater stress and suffered more anxiety and depression; however, they were not more successful at sales than the non-perfectionists. The discouragement and self-inflicted pressure characteristic of perfectionists can lead to a decrease in creativity and productivity because of self-imposed tension and fear of failure.[20]

Perfectionists want things to be easy for them, but hard for others. The story is told of a man who died and arrived at the pearly gates. Peter said to him, "You only have to meet one condition to enter heaven. Spell *love.*"

The man said, "That's easy. L-o-v-e."

"That's right!" Peter said, "Come on in. By the way, I've got to run an errand. Will you watch the gate for me? Just give each person this same test until I get back." So the man took over for Peter. He greeted a few people, then was shocked to see his wife. "What are you doing here?" he asked.

She said, "I was in a car wreck and killed on impact."

"Well," he said, "there's only one condition to get into heaven. Spell *Czechoslovakia.*"

THE PERFECTIONIST'S PLIGHT

Perfectionists share some common characteristics, as identified by David D. Burns.[21] The perfectionist believes, "I have to be perfect to be worthwhile." The problem usually begins at home with over-demanding parents who relate to their children with conditional love. As we grow up, we learn to act in certain ways in order to get people to love us. We begin to believe that love, acceptance and affirmation are dependent on a perfect performance.

Perfectionists overreact to failures and mistakes. One mistake and the perfectionist says, "I'll never get it right." "I should have done this, or I mustn't do that next time." These types of beliefs create feelings of frustration and guilt.

Perfectionists suffer from "all-or-nothing" thinking. The perfectionist may be the straight *A* student who falls apart when she makes a *B*. Or it may be the athlete who wants to quit because he had a bad performance in one game. The perfectionist is terrified of failure.

Perfectionists function in "Saint-Sinner Syndrome." They are either the best at what they do or the worst, but never in-between. The saint does everything right all the time—but when he makes a mistake, he feels like the worst sinner in history.

Perfectionists overwork and are unable to relax. Because their performance must always be perfect, needless hours of detail work consume their efforts. They have an intense need to always be in control of themselves and others. The perfectionist is, on some level, a control freak.

Perfectionists are highly self-critical; they also tend to be critical of others. Since their standards of perfection are never achieved, they live in frustration. Everyone around them becomes miserable because of the continual criticism. People who are married to perfectionists often feel as though they never do anything right and that they can never live up to their spouse's expectations.

Perfectionists aim their attention toward the future. They are always planning because they are dissatisfied with the present. They often try to correct the past and undo mistakes. They also procrastinate because of their fear of failure. All of this leads to bouts with depression stemming from their unrealistic guilt and negative self-concept.

Full-fledged perfectionists obsess about three issues: diet, time, and money. They maintain a very clean diet, are punctual with appointments and worry about financial security.

The perfectionist's greatest fears are criticism, rejection and disapproval. Such people believe that a perfect performance will insulate them from these painful experiences. Something I've heard that perfectionists should remember is this: "At age 20, we worry about what others think of us. At 40, we don't care what they think of us. At 60, we discover they haven't been thinking about us at all!"

GET OFF THE TREADMILL

Perfectionism runs contrary to a life of faith. Faith in God requires us to trust God so that we don't have to be in control. God runs the universe, not us; our job is to rest in His sovereignty.

God runs the universe, not us; our job is to rest in His sovereignty.

Under perfectionism, the concept of grace turns to legalism, and faith turns to self-righteousness. Yet the Christian life is one of a simple, powerful faith in Who Jesus is and what He accomplished for us at the cross and the resurrection. Living by faith is the end of our striving for salvation and the beginning of our resting in the finished work of Jesus.

The answer to perfectionism is faith; and I believe the highest pinnacle of faith is resting in God. We do not have to work for our salvation; we do not have to do penance to gain forgiveness. We don't even have to earn eternal life by our good works outweighing the bad. We can only receive God's gift of salvation by faith. It is in trusting, not trying, that we are saved. When we live by faith, we enter God's rest. The last words of Jesus from the cross were, *"It is finished."* We don't have to add anything to the finished work of Jesus on the cross. He alone, without our help, has provided forgiveness for our sins and the way to eternal life.

My own struggle with perfectionism began to end when I really understood one powerful statement: *"Therefore, since we have been justified through faith, we have peace with God through our Lord Jesus Christ"* (Romans 5:1). To be *justified* is to be declared righteous in God's sight. When you come into an understanding of this biblical truth, you will begin to enjoy peace with God, peace with yourself and peace with others. The perfectionist is never at peace with himself or others because of the relentless pursuit of perfection. But faith enables you to rest in what God has done for you.

Righteousness is a gift God gives us because we receive what Jesus did for us at the cross. Righteousness is not a work; it is a gift. Let that truth sink in. We tend to think of righteousness as us doing everything right. But we don't do everything right. We cannot make ourselves right with God because we have sinned against Him. We can only come to the foot of the cross, confess our sins and our inability to make ourselves righteous and receive God's gift of righteousness and the promise of eternal life. When we do, we will be at peace. Listen to this incredible insight into the cross: *"How much more will those who receive God's abundant provision of grace and of the gift of righteousness reign in life through the one man, Jesus Christ"* (Romans 5:17).

If you can rest in the fact that you have eternal life, you will be able to relax about all the things in this life that make you anxious. Think about this. If you don't have to worry about dying, then you certainly don't have to worry about living. We need to take the same faith we have about eternal life and use it to face the challenges of daily life.

Too often we find ourselves caught up in a performance relationship with God. We think He cares for us based on what we say and do and think. Our outward actions become the test of how close we are to God. The only way out is to understand who we are in Christ. God doesn't relate to us on the basis of our performance, good works or self-righteousness. He relates to us on the basis of who Jesus is in us and who we are in Christ. This is Paul's point when he says, *"You have been given fullness in Christ"* (Colossians 2:10).

Note the word *given*, not *earned*. The word *fullness* means completion. Some false teachers in the early church made people feel spiritually inadequate. These Gnostics said that salvation does not come by faith, but rather by attaining some mystical, secret knowledge of spiritual things. But Paul tells us that *"in* [Christ] *are hidden all the treasures of wisdom and knowledge"* (Colossians 2:3). We are sufficient in Christ. We are complete in Christ. He really is all we need.

Get off the treadmill of performing for God's love and man's approval and accept who you are as a child of God. God has gifted you and made you adequate. Enjoy your position of righteousness before God. Know that the cross was the place where the great exchange occurred. *"God made him who had no sin to be sin for us, so that in him we might become the righteousness of God"* (Second Corinthians 5:21). Say to yourself, "I am the righteousness of God." Not because of your perfect performance, but because of the perfect provision of Jesus on the cross for your sins and mine. That's the answer to perfectionism.

PROGRESSION, NOT PERFECTION

Seek progression, not perfection. A baseball season is considered a winning season if a team's wins outnumber its losses ... by one game. That's how we need to start measuring our success. Success is not a perfect performance; it's having one more win than our losses! That's a standard we can all reach! No one can have continually perfect performance. You see, the whole notion of perfectionism is neurotic and unhealthy.

Now, someone may say, "Doesn't Jesus tell us, *'Be perfect, therefore, as your heavenly Father is perfect'*?" (Matthew 5:48) Let's look at this. The word for "perfect" in this passage is *teleo,* meaning "to finish, fulfill and mature." Jesus is actually speaking here of being mature in love and loving others as God loves us. It is a word that describes the slow, ongoing process of maturity. Paul also says, *"our prayer is for your perfection,"* and instructs us to *"aim for perfection"* (Second Corinthians

13:9, 11; see also Ephesians 4:12-13). The word translated "perfection" in these two passages is *katartisis,* which means to restore, to mend, or to make fit, speaking of making good our deficiencies. So much for the Bible saying we ought to be perfect! God directs us to rest in His perfect provision in giving His Son to save us and to then grow and develop into the people we are capable of being.

I once heard an announcer on a Christian radio station talking about the Christian life as a striving for perfection. She added, "We aren't always perfect." I laughed out loud in the car when I heard that. Are we ever perfect?

Is this what we think the Christian life is—wavering back and forth between perfect days and imperfect days? No! Christ is our only perfection. We are only complete in Him!

I heard another Christian teacher mention "the human side of us." But that's the only side we have! We don't have a divine side. True, we are made in God's image. But we are not divine. The goal of salvation and the work of God's grace in us is not to transform us from humanity to divinity, but to make us more fully human. Sin makes us less than human. One early church leader got it right when he said, "The glory of God is a human being who is fully alive."

The secret of a life of significance is not perfection; it is dependence on God. *"We have this treasure in jars of clay"* (Second Corinthians 4:7). You don't have to be perfect before God can use you. If God could only work in this world through perfect people, He would have nothing to work with. Present yourself to God as a jar of clay. "Lord, pour into me and I will pour out to others."

Strive for excellence, and accept failure as a part of growth. Winston Churchill defined success as going from one failure to another without losing one's enthusiasm. To fail is not to be a failure—it's to be human. Try to get used to failure; it's going to be your constant guide in this life. Minimize it whenever you can, learn from it ... but get used to it.

When failures discourage you, remember that ...

... Henry Ford failed to put a reverse gear in his first car.

... Thomas Edison failed in 2,000 experiments before he finally invented the light bulb.

... The first time Benjamin Disraeli spoke before Parliament, members hissed him into silence and laughed when he said, "Though I sit down now, the time will come when you will hear of me."

... Abraham Lincoln lost nine elections for political office and failed in business twice before finally being elected President.

... Albert Einstein was dismissed from school because he lacked interest in his studies, failed an entrance exam to a school in Zurich and was later fired from his job as a tutor.

... Beethoven's music teacher, the brilliant John Albrecht Berger, said he would never compose any worthwhile music because he failed to follow the rules of musical composition.

... When Bob Dylan performed at a high school talent show, his classmates booed him off the stage. Today his songs are among the most popular works as sung by other artists.

... W. Clement Stone, successful insurance company executive and founder of *Success* magazine, was a high school dropout.

... Michael Jordan failed to make the junior varsity basketball team when he tried out. Later the school principal told him to consider enlisting in the Air Force Academy after high school, since that would be his best option for a career.

Jude, the half brother of Jesus, tells us to *"keep yourselves in God's love"* (Jude 21). It's easy to move out of love and into perfectionism, fear and inadequacy. Remember, the only cure for perfectionism is the love of God. We strive for excellence because we are loved—not in order to gain love. True spirituality is a life of love. We receive love from God and we release it to others. Somehow in the process we even learn to love ourselves.

The story is told of a court painter who painted a portrait of Oliver Cromwell. But Cromwell was afflicted with warts on his face. Thinking he would please the military leader, the painter omitted the warts. When Cromwell saw the painting, he said, "Take it away! And paint me, warts and all!" Even as we grow in the image of Jesus, we need to remember that we reflect His image—in spite of our warts and all.

FOOD FOR THOUGHT

1. Describe the lifestyle and thinking of the perfectionist. We are all perfectionists at some time; how much of a perfectionist are you?
2. Explain what is meant by this statement: "If you don't have to worry about dying, then you certainly don't have to worry about living."
3. What steps can you take to become less perfectionistic?

END NOTES

1. Shelly E. Taylor, *Biobehavioral Pattern Used by Women to Manage Stress*, Psychological Review 107, 411-29 (July 2000).

2. National Opinion Research Center survey cited in a sermon by Rabbi Janet Marder, "In Times of Stress," March 1, 2002.

3. Myers, David G., *The Pursuit of Happiness* (New York: Avon, 1992).

4. Megan Othersen Gorman, *Handle Stress Like an Expert,* Reader's Digest, 101-103 (May 1999).

5. Norman Vincent Peale, *The Power of Positive Thinking* (New York: Fawcett, 1987), 123.

6. Elisabeth Kubler-Ross, *On Death and Dying* (New York: Touchstone, 1969).

7. As told in *Bits and Pieces,* 14-15 (April 23, 1998).

8. Gary Sumner, *Untreated Depression Results in Lost Workplace Productivity,* The Atlanta Business Chronicle (November 13, 1998).

9. Jerry Grillo, *The High Cost of Depression*, Georgia Trend, 29-40 (March 2003).

10. David Brent, M.D., *Suicide in Youth*, National Alliance on Mental Illness (June 2003).

11. Archives of General Psychiatry, 62, 409-416 (April 2005).

12. As related by D. James Kennedy in his sermon, "The Spiritual State of the Union '93," Coral Ridge Ministries.

13. Gerald Corey, *Theory and Practice of Group Counseling* (Monterey: Brooks-Cole Publishing, 1981), 319-322.

14. Ten Boom, Corrie, *Tramp for the Lord* (Grand Rapids, MI: Baker Book House, 1974).

15. C. Austin Miles, "In the Garden" (Rodeheaver Co., 1940).

16. Jeanie Daniel Duck, *The Change Monster* (New York: Crown Business, 2001).

17. Adapted from Carolyn Kleiner Butler, *50 Ways to Fix Your Life*, U.S. News and World Report (December 27, 2004; January 3, 2005).

18. William Bridges, *Transitions* (Reading, PA: Addison-Wesley Publishing Co., 1995) 89-150.

19. Normal Vincent Peale, *Enthusiasm Makes the Difference* (Englewood Cliffs, N.J.: Prentice Hall, Inc., 1967) 33-34.

20. David D. Burns, *Aim for Success, Not Perfection*, Reader's Digest, 71-74 (March 1985).

20. Ibid.

ABOUT THE AUTHOR

Dr. David Cooper, an active speaker and writer, has a love for preaching the gospel of Christ in a down-to-earth style. His preaching and teaching ministry aims to make the Bible relevant and interesting to everyone. His personal philosophy for life and ministry is this: "For to me, to live is Christ" (Philippians 1:21).

Dr. Cooper's passion for ministry includes not only the teaching of the Word, but also counseling, benevolent work, care for children around the world, world missions and a music ministry that seeks to bring hope in Christ to the world. Dr. Cooper serves in various capacities with national and international ministries to further these aspects of ministry.

In addition to pastoring Mount Paran Church, Dr. Cooper serves as the Vice Chairman on the Board of Directors and as an adjunct professor in counseling at the Psychological Studies Institute in Atlanta, teaching the integration of psychology and Christian theology. He holds a Bachelor of Arts in Psychology from Lee University; a Master of Education in Counseling from the University of Georgia; and a Doctor of Ministry from Erskine Theological Seminary.

Dr. Cooper's inspirational teaching is featured on the daily radio program *Discover Life* throughout the metro-Atlanta area and northern Georgia. He is a featured motivational speaker for business and civic organizations, and his teaching ministry is also featured on Mount Paran's website at www.mountparan.com.

Dr. Cooper and his wife Barbie live in Atlanta with their two children, David Paul and Charlsi Lynn.

Contact the Author

Dr. David C. Cooper

2055 Mt. Paran Road

Atlanta, GA 30327

(877)687-2726

Website:

www.sermonsonthemount.com